THE
DO-IT-YOURSELF
DIRECT MAIL
HANDBOOK

THE DO-IT-YOURSELF DIRECT MAIL HANDBOOK

by Murray Raphel & Ken Erdman

THE MARKETERS BOOKSHELF

Book design by Bernard Schleifer

Manufactured in the United States of America

2   3   4   5   6   7   8   9   10

ISBN 0-939951-01-0

Library of Congress Catalog Card Number: 86-63913

To those who own and operate a small business.
You're one of us.

So we share with you some ideas, techniques and concepts of the most successful way to market, advertise and promote your business:
Direct Mail.

MURRAY RAPHEL
KEN ERDMAN

Contents

PART ONE:

PLANNING THE PACKAGE

PART TWO:

PRODUCING THE PACKAGE

PART THREE:

POSTING THE PACKAGE

Foreword

D IRECT MAIL IS basically a sales message delivered by mail.
It's a person-to-person, company-to-company, highly identified medium that can pinpoint its audience, personalize its message, and measure the results through orders or inquiries returned to the sender. A medium that is truly the message!

The direct mail piece or package can employ every aspect of creative advertising. Copy can be long or short, graphics can include line drawings, photographs and full-color illustrations. Envelopes, letters and brochures can be designed in almost every imaginable size, shape and color. Specialities, gifts and premiums can be included to provide intrigue. The spoken word via thin plastic records adds the dimension of sound, and even scented papers are available to take advantage of the sense of smell.

Direct mail may be the most versatile of all the media.

Through mailing list selection, both customers and prospects can be segmented into a wide variety of categories including age, sex, occupation, household income, auto ownership, business and charitable interests and even "lifestyle" as suggested through magazine subscriptions and other clues.

These highly defined segments of customers and prospects enable both the copywriter and artist to tailor their mailing to the particular interest of the audience selected. *Direct Mail* is a targeted medium.

Unlike most other media, Direct Mail results are very measurable. Your mailing can seek orders, ask for inquiries or solicit contributions. By your returns shall you know your results. If you send out 10,000 letters and 1,000 customers respond, you have a 10 percent response—it's that simple.

Contrary to what many people mistakenly believe, direct mail makes a real contribution to the public, the Government and industry. Direct Mail frequently eliminates the middle man, reducing the price of both goods and services. Direct Mail makes possible many charitable services through monies raised by mail solicitations.

The convenience of armchair shopping is made especially helpful to both the handicapped and the harried.

Businesses and the professions are kept constantly current on new products, processes, materials and services through business-to-business mail.

Politicians use Direct Mail to campaign and solicit campaign funds. They also use it to keep constituents informed. The Government has substantial budgets for Direct Mail as a very effective recruiting tool for all of the military services. Government supply facilities go to the mails regularly to seek bids and quotations for their every need.

And what about the Postal Service? Are those stories about "junk mail" really true?

In my book there's no such thing as "junk mail." All mail is valuable to someone. But some mail like some newspaper advertising or radio and TV commercials are disliked by some people, especially if the contents insult your intelligence or are an affront to one's reason. We humans enjoy *good* information no matter where it comes from. This is especially so if it's information that benefits us in some way.

What makes good information even more interesting when it comes direct mail is the convenience of getting it directly into your home or office and of having the opportunity to read it on *your schedule* rather than on someone else's programmed schedule.

Now there is a how-to-do-it-yourself Direct Mail book for the small business: the banker, barber, beauty shop operator, manufacturer, retailer —the thousands of different types of small businesses that make up 80 percent of *all* businesses in the U.S.

Now they will know how to use a powerful advertising tool not only for their own customers but future customers as well.

Only about 400,000 out of six million businesses in the U.S. have a customer data base. Since Direct Mail *is* a do-it-yourself medium, it makes sense to have a do-it-yourself book full of how-to-do-it instructions.

Direct Mail is an appreciated, effective, results-oriented medium. It's a medium many people can utilize *without* the aid of outside professional help. It's a medium that can produce significant results even on a do-it-yourself basis. Direct Mail really *is* advertising's best kept secret!

This publication now broadly shares this secret.

WILLIAM F. BOLGER
Former Postmaster General of the United States of America
Vice Chairman,
Gray and Company Public Communications International, Inc.
Washington, D.C.

Introduction

I T ALL BEGAN WITH a phone call from Ken.

"Make believe you're a small business, Murray," he said.

"O.K." I said, "I'm a small business . . . ."

It should be said up front that I am used to phone calls like this from Ken. Some people call and say, "Hello." Others call and say who they are. Not Ken. He begins the conversation in the middle of a story, and you have to think fast, act smart and answer quickly.

"No," he said, "you're a bank and you have assets of between 100 and 500 million dollars."

"Sounds good to me," I said.

"No. On second thought, you're a supermarket."

"A supermarket? Well, O.K. . . . ."

"Perhaps you're a small- to medium-sized manufacturer."

"Hmmmmm, all right."

"No," he said, "you're a retailer!"

"Right on!" I answered because I *am* a retailer.

"And you do a million dollars or so every year in business. Now, is that all right with you?"

"Is *what* all right? Am I a bank? A supermarket, a manufacturer, a retailer? What's this all about?"

"This," he said, "is all about direct mail advertising. How you put together a direct mail program for your business. Any business. Most are too small for an advertising agency. I recently read that most full service ad agencies require a minimum agency fee from their clients of $150,000. Or more."

"But all these businesses do other advertising, too," I reminded him.

"Yes," he agreed. "But you don't have to worry about doing your own newspaper ad because the newspaper sends a salesman. And so does the radio and the TV and the billboard and the magazine and the high school athletic program book and t-shirts for the Little League. They all send around a salesman. But who's the direct mail salesman"

Well, I had to admit, I didn't know of one . . .

"Exactly!" he cried, "because there isn't any. And yet how many times have I heard you say, 'Dollar for dollar, nothing returns as much business as Direct Mail'."

Well, if I said it, it must be right. But, I said, "I really don't want to be a . . . bank."

"Right," he said, "be what you are. A retailer who used direct mail to build a successful business. And a writer. Now, how about if we get together and write a book to help small businesses create result-producing do-it-yourself direct mail?"

"And how will our book be different from all the other direct mail books?" I asked.

"Easy," said Ken. "No complicated theory. No boring statistics. Just the easy basics. Lots of how-to- information. And case histories. And reference material, illustrations, places to go for help, all ready for the do-it-yourselfer."

"Great! How do we start?"

"By telling everyone all about direct mail. How it works. How they can do it. And how successful it is as America's best kept advertising secret . . ."

"Until now," I said.

"Right," said Ken. "Now . . . make believe you're a small business. . . ."

Preamble

How This Book Works

THIS MAY BE the first book you ever owned that can be read three different ways.

Having researched the many books available on both direct mail and direct marketing we felt most had one thing in common: they were very technical. They seemed directed to those already involved in the medium or those who had a need for detailed reference material on a daily basis.

The Do-It-Yourself Direct Mail Handbook is designed to be used and read in three different, but we hope enjoyable and practical, ways.

First, unlike most technical books, each chapter (omitting the TOOL-BOX sections) is written to be read like a novel. You'll find bits of history, nostalgia, opinion, references to the "greats" of direct marketing and their work, and many examples to help you better understand the theory presented.

Second, the book serves as a ready reference for your direct mail projects whether you re-read everything or just the chapter you need at that time.

Third, the TOOLBOX section at the end of each chapter provides more detailed information on the chapter and additional reference sources to help you to further explore the subject matter of that chapter.

Our goal for readers who have never ventured into the realm of direct mail is to enable them to produce, with the help of *The Do-It-Yourself Direct Mail Handbook,* their own successful direct mail or better monitor the efforts of their staff or agency-assigned direct mail responsibilities.

And for those who tried and said, "Direct Mail doesn't work . . . ," we will show you that direct mail *does* work—if you combine the right ingredients.

Part of the success of any business depends on the reading habits of its management. We sincerely hope this book will be read and re-read and referred to again and again and that it will become an important building block to your future successes in direct mail.

If you are looking for a premise, a theme, a conclusion we hope you reach by the time you come to the last page, it is simply this:

Dollar for dollar, nothing will return as much to your business as Direct Mail.

MURRAY RAPHEL
KEN ERDMAN

O-Kyaku-san

M ORE THAN 30,000 died in the U.S. last year. Each had a brief notice in the hometown paper and an even briefer funeral. Those who attended were surprised how few were there from the hundreds of friends and acquaintances made through the years. A few months later few remembered what happened when . . . or even the name. And yet each of the 30,000 was a part of the community at one time. Alive, exciting. And now they are gone.

Next year another 30,000 or so will again silently fold their tents and disappear.

Each one was . . . a business.

Most businesses fail in the first three years. Those that make it past the five-year mark have a fifty-fifty chance of success.

The struggle, however, is never ending. The passing years mean the roots grow deeper and stronger, but there are new threats internally (management, personnel, merchandising) or externally (the neighborhood changes, the shopping district moves, a new product eliminates an old).

Like people, businesses require attention. Because a business *is* like a person.

In his book *Minding the Store,* retailer Stanley Marcus tells of the beginnings of his highly successful Neiman-Marcus department store saying, "My father always said our business was a member of the family."

It's true.

You are around at the birth and watch the growth. You suffer the defeats and rejoice in the triumphs. You see the physical changes through the years and watch maturity settle in. You see the expansion in size and structure and respect in the community.

You are so closely identified with one another that people believe you think exactly alike. That's understandable. The two of you are together for

xvii

so many hours each day, some wonder if you are really one and the same person.

You are not. You each have your own identity. And though many of your thoughts, ideas, directions and plans are similar, you each have your own individual personalities. You will sometimes find the things you hesitate to do, your business does quickly. And vice versa.

Your business, oftentimes, is not only a member of your family but also sometimes your closest friend.

Through the years, those in your community find it difficult to understand that your business and you can really be two different people. That each develops his or her own personality.

Think about it for a minute. If someone asks you to describe a business in your town, you would use the same adjective to describe a neighbor: "Kind, courteous, friendly, cares about people . . ." Or "cold, uncaring, stay away from them."

How does this "personality" come about? How do you communicate your businesses's individuality to the customer?

Think about restaurants where you have dined. Some you cannot wait to bring friends to, to share the experience. Other places you advise friends not to go for many reasons. Near the top of the reasons-why list is the "attitude the restaurant has." Not the owner. The "restaurant."

Successful businesses understand this philosophy. They work toward developing the personality of their business. They create an ambiance that is warm, comfortable and makes people want to come back again. And again. And again.

One way to create that ambiance is to make sure the people who work in your business understand this sensitive, invisible, difficult-to-explain "feeling" that becomes part of the environment when customers come to call.

In a Japanese department store you are referred to as "O-kyaku-san."

Translated, this means you are a "visitor to my home."

Isn't that how you want your customers to feel about your business? That they are "visitors to your home"? Because your business is a member of your family.

How do you convey this same feeling *outside* your business?

It is difficult (perhaps impossible) to create this message in general advertising (newspaper, magazine, radio). But it is very possible, in fact the reason for direct mail advertising.

In direct mail you clone yourself for the price of a postage stamp and tuck yourself into the mailboxes of your customers (and potential customers).

This was the situation facing Australian Mutual Provident Society (AMP), the largest insurance company in Australia. Each of their 3,500 agents serviced nearly 1,000 personal customers. It took, on average, three *years* to see each one. Was there a way they could "see" them more often?

Yes. Direct mail.

Today AMP has Direct Response centers all over Australia, and their marketing manager calls it "the most effective advertising medium we have ever used."

They are not alone. Direct mail is the fastest growing advertising medium throughout the world! One of the major reasons: It pinpoints your customer. And it is personal. Direct mail is the most *personal* of all advertising mediums. It is a me-and-thee approach. Like . . . a visitor in one's home.

Forget to place an ad in a newspaper or run a commercial on TV or radio and few if any of your customers will call or care.

But forget to send a customer a direct mail piece and you will soon have a irate call saying who they are and asking why you forgot to tell them of the special offer/promotion/message you told others about, and, "Don't you want me to come to your store [or business] to buy your merchandise?"

They are insulted.

Your mailings will be immediately recognizable because they should "look like" your business. We once forgot to put our store's name on an outside envelope. It was mentioned only once buried in the inside copy (no, not on purpose, in error). People came in to buy the products advertised. We asked them how they knew the mailer they received was from us. They said, "Why, it looked like your store."

Be proud, possessive and positively passionate about maintaining your business's individual identity. Direct mail will do that for you.

In the following chapters you will see how it works for you. Try it. You'll like it. If nothing else, it will increase your life expectancy so your business won't be one of the 30,000 whose obituary appears in next year's newspapers.

PART ONE:

PLANNING THE PACKAGE

1
Direct Mail: Advertising's Best-Kept Secret

Where It Came From

THERE WAS A LOT OF excitement in the Indus Valley that runs between India and Pakistan when the citizens first heard that an organized message delivery system was starting in business.

No, it was not United Parcel Service or even the India/Pakistan mail system. It was a private business concern that thought it would be profitable and informative to send messages from one tribe to another.

It didn't make the papers and you never saw it on TV because it happened about 4,000 B.C.

The roots of direct mail go back thousands of years and include messages written in hieroglyphics on papyrus and fabric sent throughout the Egyptian Kingdom. (A more recent occurrence, about 3,000 B.C.).

Nat Ross writes in his *History of Direct Marketing* that direct mail began with the Assyrians, Babylonians and Persians using clay tablets and cuneiform inscriptions in the year 2,000 B.C. A Babylonian clay wrapper, perhaps the very first envelope, dates back to that year.

Two important inventions in the history of direct mail are moveable type (Gutenberg in 1437) and the typewriter patented in 1714.

Although the printing press made possible production of handbills announcing the sale of various products and services, there were three important events in the 1860s in the U.S. that brought about the advertising mail revolution: (1) Penny postage, introduced in 1863; (2) the origin of three classes of mail; and (3) the marketing of the typewriter in 1874.

Among the early pioneers in direct mail were Benjamin Franklin, the unofficial first Postmaster General before the independence of the Colonies. Franklin, a printer, published catalogs of books and sold his famous *Poor Richard's Almanac* by mail.

For more than twenty years Americans sold merchandise person to person or door to door. The customer either went to the business or someone brought the business to them.

Things haven't changed much. The customer still goes to the business or the business comes to them—but today, more often than not, through the mail.

Although predated by seed, patent medicine, sporting goods and abbreviated general merchandise catalogs in the mid 1800s, it was Montgomery Ward's mail order business started in 1872 and the Sears, Roebuck partnership established in 1887 that gave the real impetus to the direct media.

Soon the word spread, and a few years later, Joseph Spiegel, advertising furniture at low prices in Chicago, began to find orders in his morning mail. The letters were ignored until his son Arthur set up a special department just to handle the mail orders. A few years later they had a full service mail department.

America was not alone. In 1860, Aristide Boucicaut in France took items from the Bon Marché store and offered them through the mail.

In Germany, the Post Annoncen Bureau in the Schommerstrasse offered small advertisements on postcards. They were so convinced it would work, the first offer was free.

By 1900, insurance companies were using the German mails and still are. In Belgium they started to sell seeds and bulbs through the mail. And still do.

As the years went on, direct mail continued to grow. But there was one underlying concept that made it work: they promised the relationship that existed in the store would also exist through the mail. In fact, they guaranteed it would! Here's why . . .

In The Beginning . . .

A customer was treated as an individual.

There was no mass merchandising, marketing, advertising. The men and women who settled America brought their Old World techniques and talents to the new land. The tailor, the printer, the potter, the tinsmith even the farmer served customers one at a time.

Even as the country grew, most sales took place in small stores that sold small quantities to small groups of people. Face to face, one on one.

The customers returned because they were satisfied with the merchandise they bought and with the merchants from whom they bought it.

Shortly before World War II, there developed in this country a "mass market." Suddenly chain drugstores, chain supermarkets, chain shoe stores. chain everything began to appear serving a total market rather than an individual market.

As this mass marketing grew, so did the clamor for attention to this market.

Daily, the average person sees 300 or more advertising messages in print. They hear another three messages every few minutes they listen to the radio. They watch another five messages every fifteen minutes the TV is on. The clamour to capture attention becomes so loud it is amazing *any* message makes its way to anyone anytime.

What happened: Society moved from a personal society to an impersonal society. What was good for one became good for all. Suddenly the word "Occupant" appeared on mailings delivered to households all over the U.S. It made no difference *who* the occupant was, as long as there was an occupant.

But whenever a pendulum swings too far in one direction, there is a counterbalance set into motion. And the consumer wakes up one morning and resents being classified as "everyone" instead of someone. The customer is ready, willing and anxious to respond to the merchant, manufacturer, businessman, baker, grocer who talks to him or her as an *individual.*

A recent survey said more people (63 percent) look forward to the mail than to such daily activities as watching TV, hobbies, eating dinner and sleeping.

When asked in a recent study what factors influenced a customer's decision to buy, 5,000 people said the first consideration was *confidence.* Second, quality. Third, selection. Fourth, service. *Price was fifth.* In fact, only 14 percent of the respondents listed price as the first reason for making a purchase or for selecting a business where they prefer to buy or shop.

That's why this book is important to you. It recaptures that original personal relationship through direct mail.

Direct mail is the most personal of all advertising.

It is a one-on-one, me-and-thee approach . . . directed to a particular person at a particular address (not Occupant).

Dollar for dollar nothing will return as much business as direct mail.

Because you show the customer you care. Because you are talking to him and her as a person. Because it is simply going back to how it worked (and worked well) when . . .

In the beginning . . . a customer was treated as an individual.

How It Works

Within the past few months I bought a $500 air conditioner, a life insurance policy, a $20,000 car and a $50 pair of shoes.

Following these sales, I heard from none of the businesses—except my shoe salesman. He thanked me for coming in to buy and hoped I would "receive much comfort" and remember him the next time I wanted another pair of shoes. Or perhaps I had a friend who . . .

There's something wrong here.

I called each of the retailers (except the shoe store) and asked if they ever thought of writing thank-you letters after the sale. These are actual answers:

The air conditioner dealer: "I don't think we ever did that. Well, once in a while our financing company writes a letter to all the people they carry on their books." (What for? He wasn't sure.). "Listen, we know it's a good idea and I know you're going to ask why we don't do it, and the answer is, I guess we just never got around to it. There's so much to do in this business . . ."

The life insurance salesman: "Sending a thank-you letter is the best thing I ever did.

"Absolutely. I stopped about eight or nine months ago. I'm so backed up with all the paperwork that I just don't have the time anymore. But I'll tell you something—from the customer's point of view it was terrific. I used to get a big response. I've got to get back to that sometime . . ."

The automobile dealer: "Are you kidding? Why that's the first thing we do. The day the car is delivered, the salesman sits down and writes a thank-you letter right away. Positively . . ."

Well, that was a month ago. No letter yet.

What's happening?

The small-business person—that's the people in about 80 percent of the businesses in this country—knows the buzz words of successful businesses are "service" and "taking care of the customer."

Now, the smaller independently owned businesses can also show the customer they appreciate their business . . . in an advertising medium.

And this is where direct mail stands alone. Literally.

There is no confusion with other ads in the papers, on the radio or seen on TV. Because . . . direct mail *stands alone*. It carries your message to your customer with no competition.

And it *is* read (see Direct Mail Fiction & Fact at the end of this chapter).

A generally ignored fact of business: It is far, far easier to attract more dollars from the customer you already have than from the customer you do *not* have.

How do you do that? Direct mail.

Our local florist recently celebrated its 100th year in business. The shop has one person responsible to send out reminders on who-sent-what-to-whom last year at this time and the florist will be glad to repeat the order if you simply call . . .

The customer contact that made the business successful through the years still works.

No wonder the business is still going strong after 100 years.

Direct Mail Fiction and Fact

Fiction	*FACT*
Nobody reads direct mail. They throw it away unopened.	Eight out of 10 direct mail pieces are opened and at least looked at. Direct mail is the best-read advertising medium.
Most direct mail is just thrown in the mailbox, addressed to an anonymous "occupant."	Nine out of 10 direct mailers are addressed to a specific household member
Most people don't want to receive direct mail ads.	About 72 percent like receiving mail.
Most direct mail is coupons that are just thrown away.	If you add up the coupons *and* post cards *and* small packages, the total is about 3 percent.
Why do we have to subsidize this advertising for the post office?	Third-class mail is the *only* class of mail that pays for itself. One out of four postal workers depends on direct mail for his livelihood.
Mailboxes are clogged every week with direct mail ads.	The national average is three pieces per week.
If most people had the chance, they'd take their names off mailing lists.	The Direct Marketing Association runs periodic ads in national publications offering to take names off the mailing lists of its 1,700 member companies. Or to put names *on* lists. So far, those wanting to receive MORE mail out-number those who want to receive less.
It is awfully risky to buy through the mail.	Mail-order volume depends on repeat business. They must have satisfied customers to stay alive. (Notice how direct mailers stress their guarantee?) And, the federal government has very strict regulations on offers that use the U.S. mails.
You can't sell expensive things through the mail.	Don't tell Sharper Image or all those folks selling computer and high-tech items. They know you can!

The Three Ways to Increase Your Business
And the One Medium That Works in All Three

There are three ways you can increase your business.
And each of them involves customers:

1. Customers who are new to your store or business.
2. Customers who spend more money when they arrive at your store or business.
3. Customers who come more often to your store or business.

If only there was one advertising medium that brought in new customers, had present ones spend more when they arive and made them come more often.

There is: *Direct mail.*

And we start . . . on the next page.

2
Everything Is at Sixes and Sevens

T HE PHRASE "Everything is at sixes and sevens" usually means everything is confused and messy. But in direct mail we use sixes and sevens *harmoniously* and come up with a hit.

Because . . . there are *six* ways your business can use direct mail and *seven* ways to use it successfully.

The Six Ways to Use It

1. **Order by mail for a product or service.**
2. **Ask for a salesman to call.**
3. **Bring the reader to your place of business.**
4. **Do a simple advertising job on who you are.**
5. **Do some research.**
6. **Something other than a sale.**

Let's show you how each works:

1. Order by mail for a product or service. Nothing complicated about that. Just like the words say.

- It can be a catalog you send to your customer.
- It can be an item (or items) or service you include in a monthly statement.
- It can be someone filling out a coupon in the newspaper and mailing it to you.

2. Ask for a salesman to call. You introduce a new piece of equipment. You show the product and whet the interest in a mailing piece. Now, give the prospect a chance to check a box, "Please have a salesperson call and tell me more about how this works."

Or . . . you receive a brochure from a manufacturer with fabric swatches enclosed and a letter saying why his merchandise is new and exciting. And then, "If you want to see the complete line and hear about our new plans, simply call 1-800- . . ."

Or . . . you see a bank ad in major metropolitan dailies with the headline: "We make house calls." This is a half-step ahead of the "Fill out this application and mail it today . . ." (As in number one above.)

Or . . . a supermarket offers to deliver groceries. In this age of one-on-one marketing there is a vast audience of people out there who (1) don't like to shop for food, (2) are old and infirm and simply find it too difficult to shop for food, and (3) want someone to deliver sandwich trays for their party.

Your direct mailer can have all kinds of responses: by mail, by person or by phone.

3. Bring the reader to your place of business. This is how direct mail works for many businesses, professionals and most retail stores. Those who mail catalogs see customers come into their store *with* the catalog in their hand. The customer could have ordered by mail but decided instead to see the merchandise first hand. Live. In person. Ready to buy.

This is also the best example of direct mail's greatest strength. You let your customer know something no one else knows. Something just between the two of you. This is why we say, 'Tis far, far easier to sell more to the customer you have than to sell a new customer.

This reason to use direct mail brings the customer to your store, your business, your service, your trade show because you offer them something special because well, *they* are something special: Your customer.

4. Do a simple advertising job on who you are. Some call this "institutional" advertising, letting the potential customer know who you are and what you do. Nothing wrong with that. When you have just opened for business, it *is* a good idea to let the local folks know you are in business and where you are and what you have for them to buy.

If you are a bank, send a mailer to the local businesses where you plan to open your branch bank.

If you are a supermarket, send weekly mailers to the people living in your shopping area. Tell them you have arrived, and what you have to sell. Don't forget to include some coupons to bring them in. (The mailboxes in Finland are packed every week with advertisements from competitive food stores).

Remember: the main reason people go to a certain business, bank or a specific supermarket is . . . convenience.

5. *Do some research.* Are you what you think you are? Or something else instead? One way to find out: Ask your customers.

It can be a simple "We want to serve you better" questionnaire where you list all the pro and con adjectives and ask the customers to pick and choose. ("Which adjective best describes our business to you? Check one: ☐ friendly ☐ courteous ☐ goes out of its way to help ☐ just the opposite of all those.")

Or you are thinking of taking in new merchandise. Would your customer buy these items? Ask them ahead of time.

Or: What would your customers like you to carry or make that you are not presently carrying or making?

Or: You may simply want to find out more about your customer. Either (a) who they are, or (b) what they want. We tend to think our customers are the same as we are—the same demographics (where we live, how much we earn), psychographics (what we think about), like to jog, have a mortgage, three kids, and two cars.

Sorry, not true.

There *is* a general description of who/what/where your customers are and it is probably *not* the same as who/what/where you are. It is important you know. It is best if *they* tell you.

6. *Something other than a sale.* You make an announcement about your business's address. Or new employee(s). Or a seminar you are conducting. A reason to vote for you (or your friend) in the upcoming election. A request for a contribution to your favorite charity.

Direct mail is a selling tool. But it does not have to be merchandise. It can be a thought, a concept, a commitment to a person or organization.

How about a "thank you" *after* the sale. Neiman-Marcus employees jot customers a little note thanking them for shopping with them. It's remembered and talked about to others.

Important: Each of these six reasons-for-using tells the customer more about you and your product or service and reinforces your image in the community.

Most people in business assume since they have been in business for so many years that everyone knows who they are, what they do, when they are open, where they are and why people seek them out.

Wrong.

We call this the "Curse of the Assumption." You *assume* everyone knows who you are and what you do. But one out of five people in the community in which you live change their address every year.

One of the most famous ads in American advertising history is called "The Angry Man Ad." It was published by McGraw-Hill and selected by *Advertising Age* as one of the ten best institutional ads of all time. It shows a heavy-set scowling executive sitting in a chair and staring at you. Next to him are these sentences:

I don't know who you are.
I don't know your company.
I don't know what your company stands for.
I don't know your company's record.
I don't know your company's reputation.
I don't know your company's customers.
Now . . . what is it you wanted to sell me?*

We *assume* because *we* know who we are, where we work and our spouse knows and our children know and our parents know and our nieces and nephews and cousins know—well then, everyone knows.

Not true.

But direct mail is a constant reminder to your customer not only of who you are but that you are still doing business at the same stand in the same place with the same kind of products or services.

L. L. Bean of Freeport, Maine saw their clothing, shoe and camping business increase tenfold simply because they increased their mailings to their customers from twice a year to *every* month. They discovered their customers did not want to buy the merchandise only when L. L. Bean thought they wanted to buy the merchandise. The customers wanted the merchandise all year long.†

O.K., now that you know *what* Direct Mail will do for your business, *how* should you do it?

We have read, examined, digested dozens of rules and secrets and reasons why direct mail works (See Toolbox: The Formula to End All Formulas).

Nearly forty years ago, Edward Mayer, Jr., one of the earliest writers and lecturers on direct mail said there were seven cardinal rules for direct mail success:

1. **Establish an objective.**
2. **Say what it does for the reader.**
3. **Make the layout and copy fit.**
4. **Address correctly.**
5. **Make it easy to take action.**
6. **Repeat.**
7. **Test.**

*Reproduced by permission of McGraw-Hill Magazines.
†Write for a copy of L. L. Bean's catalog, Freeport, Maine 04033

"I don't know who you are.
I don't know your company.
I don't know your company's product.
I don't know what your company stands for.
I don't know your company's customers.
I don't know your company's record.
I don't know your company's reputation.
Now—what was it you wanted to sell me?"

MORAL: Sales start **before** your salesman calls—with business publication advertising.

McGRAW-HILL MAGAZINES
BUSINESS • PROFESSIONAL • TECHNICAL

Let's take a closer look at each rule.

1. Establish an Objective.

What do you want your mailing piece to accomplish?

It is amazing how many mailing pieces never tell you what they want you to do. This information should be up front. Are you introducing a new product? Asking for an order? Want a salesman to come and explain in more detail?

Once you know what you are trying to do, the writing of the mailer will follow that direction.

2. Say What It Does for the Reader.

Direct mail answers this question far more effectively than any other advertising because it is the most *personal* of all advertising.

Let's show you how it works:

You meet an attractive woman (or man). You ask her out for dinner. You have a good time. The next day you write her a letter saying, "Thanks for an exciting and thoroughly enjoyable evening. I hope we can do it again soon. I really enjoyed being with you."

She reads your note and thinks it was rather nice of you to say those nice words and tucks the note in her pocketbook.

Now, let's assume instead of sending her a note, you take out an ad in her local newspaper. Your headline says "An open message to . . ." with her name. The ad has the same words as the letter.

Would she be complimented . . . or embarrassed?

Or . . . you contact the radio station in her home town and have the radio announcer read the same message over the air. Would she be complimented . . . or embarrassed? Her friends could easily read other meanings into the same words.

She is offended! She thinks you are terrible! She is embarrassed to see her friends!

What happened? When you wrote the same words in a letter, her reaction was warm and positive. When you put it out for all the world to see, her reaction was cold and negative.

Why? Because. Direct mail forms an emotional bond between you and your customer positively, absolutely, unattainable in any other advertising medium.

In fact, your customers look forward to receiving mail from you. Few will pick up the morning paper and look for your ad or twist the dial trying to hear your commercial ad. But most will open, read and often act on your ad if they receive it in the mail.

If a customer of ours does *not* receive a mailer that others have received, the reaction is immediate and irritated. A phone call wanting to know why we left them off the list. We apologize, blame the post office or the mailing house . . . all to no avail. We have discriminated against them, and they are mad!

It happened to the First National Bank of Wilmette, Illinois. They put together a five week direct mail program. Every Thursday morning the residents of Wilmette would receive a message from the bank advertising one of their products or services.

One week it listed all the services the bank offered. The next week it announced the bank's special hours. The fifth and last week summarized the four services and including a calling card from a bank officer.

That was all.

Or so thought the bank.

On the Thursday morning of the sixth week, the bank's phones started ringing early and continued all day long. They had a record number of incoming calls that day. When someone from the bank answered, they would hear a voice on the other end of the line saying, "I didn't get any mail from the bank today. How come?"

People like to receive mail!

3. Make the Layout and Copy Fit.

"You don't wear a tuxedo to the beach," said writer/lecturer Ed Mayer, "and you don't wear a bathing suit to a formal dinner."

If you are advertising men's work clothes, the mailing piece will not have a soft feminine look.

If you are sending a personal letter to someone, do not have it printed.

Your mailing must have a mood and feeling and image and look that is *you.*

"Every advertisement that you run is an investment in yourself," says famed advertising expert David Ogilvy. And it's true.

The typeface you choose. The color you select. The artist you employ. Each of these must work together to come up with a total concept the customer associates with you and your business.

Example: supermarkets print four color rotogravure tabloids they mail to all the households in their area. But most supermarket ads look so much alike, the customer is not sure where the mailing piece came from until they look at the name.

That was the problem facing Charley Braun in his Food Ranch supermarket in Mud Lake, Idaho. (Yes, there *is* a Mud Lake, Idaho.)

For years Charlie did the same advertising as his competitor: the four-color rotogravure 8-page tabloid mailed to every "Occupant" in his home town. The people received these mailers along with the mailers from all the other stores. Impact was small. So he tried something different. One Thanksgiving he mailed an 8½ " x 11" sheet of paper to his customers with food specials typewritten on one side. The other side said this was his "No frills" advertising. The rest of the page was left blank for children to draw pictures of turkeys and bring the sketches to the store for a prize.

Sales jumped 80 percent over previous "professional" mailings.

"When they receive one of my new mailers," says Charlie, "they know it's from me and not someone else."

4. *Address Correctly.*

This rule has two meanings.

The first is as the words say: Make sure you send your mailer to the correct address. (Remember that one out of five people in your town moves every year.) And . . . it also means to spell the name correctly. People dislike having their name misspelled.

We still have a selling letter beginning, "Dear Rapahel Murray." Backwards. And misspelled.

Followed by this clever opening line:

"I don't need to tell you how important first impressions can be."

We agreed and threw that one away!

Ken Erdman once signed a "request for more information" coupon and reversed the name and address lines. He put his city (Philadelphia) on the line set aside for "name."

To this day, Ken Erdman receives mail addressed to Phil A. Delphia and of course, beginning, "Dear Phil . . ."

Addressing correctly also calls attention to two key ingredients necessary for a successful direct mail piece. (Here it is on this one page and you thought you had to read the whole book.)

1. The list.
2. The product or service.

If you have an excellent product but advertise it to the wrong people . . .you will have few sales.

If you have an excellent mailing list but advertise an item not applicable to this group . . . you will have few sales.

What does that mean?

This: If you have a list of senior citizens and you mail them a subscription letter for the books for children in kindergarten . . . you have few sales. (Good list, bad offer.)

This: If you are selling retirement homes at a low price and you sent the offer to newlyweds . . . you will have few sales. (Good offer, bad list.)

Most people in business have a list of their customers. Milt Smolier, past president of the mailing house Names Unlimited, said, "If you have a mailing list of customers, you're in the direct mail business."

The direct mail professionals call that information a "data base." Fine. What it is is a list of your customers' names and addresses. The ones who know you, who shop with you and (most important) will open and read what you send them.

Companies sending out mailings to "Occupant" are satisfied if they receive a ½ of 1% return. (Translation: If they mail out 100,000 mailers and 500 customers show up to buy, they are happy.)

But businesses who mail to their own customers show consistent returns of 5-20% or *more*.

5. *Make It Easy to Take Action.*

Always include a "response mechanism." That means the customer can fill out and send it back to you by simply dropping a card or business-reply envelope into the mailbox. (Yes, you pay the postage. Would you pay less than a quarter to have a customer come in your front door or call on your phone ready to buy?)

Give your customers *different* ways they can buy.

The more choices you give them, the greater response.

This is a variation of a selling technique you use every day in your business called the "Not If But Which" method. You never offer a customer one shirt and ask him if he wants to buy it. You offer several and say, "Which one do you like?"

Or a choice of cars or insurance programs or computers or what-you-sell.

And so, you let your customer pay you by cash. Or check. Or charge. Or their choice of credit cards. Or calling this 800 number. Or by simply pulling off the "Yes" or "No" sticker and putting the one they want on the label. Or return card.

Now—why do businesses *pay* to find out who does *not* want to buy?

Because you want the customer *involved* with you. By taking off the "No" sticker, putting it on the reply card and writing their name and address, they show they are interested . . . but not convinced.

Now that you have them involved, how do you have them committed?

Here's how: write back to the ones who said "No."

State all the advantages one more time and then give them one *more* reason to buy.

Tests show about one out of four customers who say "No" the first time around will say "Yes" the second time around.

Always, always, always, always offer a GUARANTEE with your mailer. They must be satisfied or they can have their money back. (See Chapter 4.)

6. *Repeat!*

McGraw-Hill published a survey that says it takes a salesman an average of five calls to make the first sale.

When you add up to the approximate $200 per sale cost, this is a lot more expensive than five direct mail pieces to the same customer.

Very few salespeople make the sale the first time around. Even the best often use the first call to find out information they need for the second call.

Persistence is a key to effective selling. Which was certainly the quality of the tie salesman who called on us for four years without making a sale. "When are you going to stop coming to see us?" we asked him one time. He looked, paused, then said, "Depends on which one of us dies first."

Chase Manhattan bank sends out letters asking if you want to borrow money. There is a deadline stamped on the letter showing the latest day you can take the Chase Advantage of this offer.

The deadline passes. You have lost out. But, no . . . wait! Here is another letter from Chase. Well, really the *same* letter. But where the deadline date was, it is now crossed out in red with the phrase "Extended until . . ." and a new date a week away.

Here is still another technique called "The Publisher's Letter" because it began with book clubs.

How it works: Within your mailing piece include a folded-over note. On the outside it has a phrase similar to this: "Do not open unless you have decided *not* to buy."

When your customer opens this little note, she sees a short memo from the president of your company or a testimonial of a well-known person. Who simply can't believe she is not buying the product. And here's one more reason why you should . . .

"Publisher's Letters" in quantities of a few thousand cost less than a penny apiece to print and can increase a return by as much as 10 percent. That's 10 percent *additional*.

(Example: if you were normally having a 5 percent return, adding this little reminder increases your return to 5.5 percent. Or 10 percent more.)

7. *Test!*

This is the one unique characteristic that belongs to direct mail advertising.

You do not have to spend money on printing and postage of massive mailings until you first test to see the probable results.

Direct mail is the *only* form of advertising you can test for accuracy. Imagine asking the newspaper if your ad can be in the paper but delivered only to certain sections of your community.

Imagine telling the radio or TV salesman to broadcast your message only into certain sections of town.

"Impossible," they say. "Can't do it," they would reply.

But with direct mail you can pinpoint the customer you want, where you want and as many as you can. Or as few.

And it's measurable!

You know the results almost immediately.

If you send out 10,000 letters and 1,000 customers respond, you have a 10 percent response.

How do you *really* know how many people read the paper or heard the radio and responded?

And will your newspaper guarantee you *one percent* of their total *circulation* will respond to your ad?

If they will, place *all* your money in that newspaper.

But they will not. They cannot.

Yet you can receive a response of 10 or 20 percent *or even more* from your own mailing list, from your own customer.

In this book you will read of businesses receiving as much as *80 percent return.*

(For more information on testing see Chapter 16.) It's been said direct mail is a *what* medium not a *why* medium. If you send out 10,000 letters and you receive 1,000 orders you know *what* happened. You had a 10 percent response. But you don't necessarily know *why.* Wouldn't it be simple and easy if there was a magic formula for success?

We went to some of the top experts in direct mail and asked if they would give us their Secret Formula . . .

TOOLBOX

The Formulas to End All Direct Mail Formulas

Ponce de León left St. Augustine unhappy because he could not find the Formula for Everlasting Youth. Dr. Jekyll had a bad lunch when he whipped up a formula only to find it changed his Hyde. Those looking for the formula to make both ends meet soon discover what happens when you burn the candle at both ends.

Throughout history, people looking for the quick fix, easy solution and magic formula have, more often than not, been disappointed.

But the search continues in all walks of life, business and . . . direct mail.

Is there a magic formula, once used, that guarantees success?

Are there words, phrases, concepts, once put together, that will bring in the crowds, ring the register, fill the bank account?

Is there a way to guarantee success once the pen is to the paper, the fingers on the typewriter, the floppy disc in the computer?

Well, yes.

And then again, no.

And so there are books written, speeches given and seminars conducted on the never ending search for *why* . . . why does direct mail work when it *does* work?

And so we contacted some of the best known direct mail experts around the world. We asked them for their execlusive formula. Would they share this secret with us?

Amazingly, they all said Yes.

It's off to the lab for those not-so-secret formulas.

A I D A

*A*ttention, *I*nterest, *D*esire, *A*ction

This is seen in almost every text and best remembered by Verdi's opera of the same name: *Aida.*

Earliest publication seems to be in 1920 by Cyril Freer, advertising manager of the *Daily Mail,* according to Drayton Bird, United Kingdom

DM expert. (Here in the colonies, credit is given to E. K. Strong in his 1925 book, *The Psychology of Selling.*) Freer's book, *The Inner Side of Advertising* said a good sales letter should include:

"The opening which should attract the reader's *Attention* and induce him to read.

"The description and explanation should hold their *Interest* by causing him to picture the proposition in his or her mind.

"The argument should create the *Desire* for the article offered for sale. And . . .

"The climax which makes it easy for the reader to order and assures that *Action* by causing him to act at once."

K I S S

Keep It Short and Simple

Short sentence. Short paragraphs. Words of one and two syllables. All easily understood and quickly acted upon. The simplest direct mail package seems to, more often than not, outpull the more complicated packages.

(A variation of this phrase came from the frustrated head of agency who could not convince his Ph.D. English copywriter that intellectualism in writing did not sell merchandise. In frustration, he yelled out his own interpretation of the formula saying, "*Keep It Simple, Stupid!*")

P P P P

Picture, Promise, Proof, Push

It was nearly thirty years ago that Henry Hoke, father of the publisher of *Direct Marketing* magazine, wrote a booklet for the Bureau of Business Management at the University of Illinois. The title: *How to Use the Mails for Sales.*

The formula Hoke gave us then (that still works today) is this one: Start your message by having the customer *picture* your offer. You then *promise* this picture will become a reality if they simply buy your product. For *proof* here is what other folks—just like you—say about how much they enjoy this merchandise. And so, hurry, quick, now, at-once, the *push* is on for you to order.

D D P C

Dramatic, Descriptive, Persuasive, Clinch

Mystery-story writers capture the reader's attention with something dramatic. So do the opening paragraphs of front page features in the *Wall Street Journal.* They begin with a sentence or two to capture your interest.

Then, describe in more detail, the dramatic beginning. Now, switch gears and become persuasive by offering benefits to be received and end by clinching the sale.

R I C

*R*eadership, *I*nvolvement, *C*ommitment

This is the technique used effectively by talented Joe Sugarman of JS&A Sales. He captures readership immediately with a short attention-grabbing opening sentence. He then involves the customer with his story and concludes with a giant 800 telephone number at the end for the order. Sugarman pulls them off the fence and onto the phone. It's a playback of the last scene in a Gregory Peck movie. Facing down an enemy, Peck turns to a third party in the room who must choose which side to take. Seeing the indecision, Peck tells them there comes a time in every person's lift when they have to make a decision. And he yells to him: *"Commit!"*

R F M

*R*ecency, *F*requency, *M*onetary

These are often called the three most important factors in customer information. The trio were the first to find their way onto computer floppy discs.

They mean what they say. Recency is first because it tells you the most recent date the customer bought from you.

The next, Frequency, tells you how often they buy—the more frequent, the more loyal, the more valuable.

The last, Monetary, tells you how much they spend either on the latest order or during the time they have been on your list.

The Cy Frailey Formula

Star, Chain and Hook

When teaching at Northwestern University in the late 1930s, Cy Frailey taught his class this concept:

Close your eyes. Picture a star. Then several links of chain running down from the star. Look, there, at the bottom of the chain there's a large hook!

The star represents the attention or picture or drama. The chain is a series of connecting links (interest, desire, promise, proof, description) and the hook is the request for action.

OK, those are the best known and most used formulas.

Now, are there other formulas out there, kept hidden and guarded through the years by some of the best-known practitioners of our craft? And, would they, upon request, reveal their sources?

The answer was yes and yes.

There *were* other formulas out there. And the winners *were* willing to share.

Let us remind you up front that *books* have been written on direct mail formulas. In picking and choosing these, we set the criteria of nonduplication and, for the most part, from writers working today with consistent records of success.

Here they are in alphabetical order.

ED BURNETT
Ed Burnett Consultants

Ed came up with his version of the Marx brothers: Dido, Gigo, Nino and Rafo. He says the computer world has spawned a whole new list of formulas to be observed and paid attention to:

They include:

DIDO   *D*uplication *In*, *D*uplication *Out*

GIGO   *G*arbage *In*, *G*arbage *Out*

NINO   *N*ot *In*, *N*ot *Out*

RAFO   What you do when you forget to NINO. You go back and *R*esearch *A*nd *F*ind *Out*.

In other words: the computer only gives back to you what you give it. Not far different from the age-old dictum of you only get out of something what you put into it . . .

RAY CONSIDINE
Considine & Associates

The Salesman from the West reminds us there is nothing that successfully replaces his *Four-mula for Success* with customers or clients.

Like a four-a-day vitamin schedule: take four of one, or one of each, or any mix. "It always works," says this direct marketing doctor.

Prescription: Four Notes (handwritten). Four telephone calls (brief).

Four PC's (no, no, not IBM's but *P*ersonal *C*ontacts asking for referrals). Four AFTO's (in itself, *another* formula "*A*sk *F*or *T*he *O*rder").

The secret, Raymond says, is there is no secret. Direct Marketers who are successful always stay in touch with their best customers.

KEN ERDMAN
Co-author

Not to be outdone, co-author, Ken wanted his "Chicken Pox" formula included. It works like this: after you have written your letter or copy, go over it carefully and draw a red circle around all of the personal pronouns; I, we, us, ours, my. Then look for exaggerated words; biggest, best, most, etc. Then if your work seems to suffer from chicken pox you need a quick cure.

Change the red-circled pronouns to the words "you" or "yours" and try to tone down the exaggerated claims.

Look again. If the rash has disappeared, you are on your way to healthy copy.

KENNETH GOODE

Herb Ahrend reminds us of Goode's Glass, Magnet, Escalator secret to successful direct marketing.

Make your proposition as clear as *glass,* as attractive as a *magnet* and as easy to execute as riding an *escalator.*

FREEMAN GOSDEN
Smith-Hemmings-Gosden

"I don't use the formulas 'cause I can never remember the letters . . .", says Freeman Gosden. But he *does* remember *numbers!* His most successful: the 40-40-20 formula.

40% marketing. Who you are. What product or service you offer. What is the price or "deal."

40% audience: The right list (from the more than 35,000 available). Advertising in the right media at the right time.

20% creativity: Copy. Theme. Format. Graphics. Paper. Envelopes. Color. Postage. And more.

His conclusion: get the first two right and the third falls into place.

ROSE HARPER
The Kleid Company

The president of The Kleid List Company admits she has been trying to create a winning formula for a long time. She called her staff together and had them vote. Their choice: T A P.

They agreed on the initials. But not on the words. The two choices (take your pick): *T*est, *A*nalyze, *P*roject. Or *T*est, *A*nalyze, *P*rogress.

RICHARD HODGSON
Writer, Speaker on Direct Marketing Techniques

The man who wrote the book on successful mail order advertising says there are two Hodgson formulas:

1. Don't use formulas.
2. Hire someone who knows enough not to use a formula.

Copy written by a formula is like a horse created by a committee. It turns out to be a camel, says Hodgson.

He admits all the experts have formulas, and since he *is* an expert, he does say there are four key words that form the cornerstone of successful direct marketing. Each of these words "should be preceded by the adjective, 'perceived,' " says Hodgson. "The real facts are not often as important as what the potential customer perceives to be the facts." Here are the four words:

1. *Availability:* Does the reader think your product is not easily accessible in a nearby shop?
2. *Authority:* Testimonials from well-known people/organizations. History of how long you've been in business. A reason-why the reader thinks your product is superior.
3. *Value:* The customer must feel they are receiving something of value for them. This has nothing to do with your mark-up. But rather what the merchandise means to them in terms of their needs.
4. *Satisfaction.* The well-known "guarantee" you see in all the direct mail catalogs.

ED NASH
President, Ed Nash Direct

"Aha," says Ed, "so *that's* how formulas come about. People like me don't want to be left out of books by people like you . . ."

He likes the AIDA formula as taught to him by Vic Schwab. But his personal favorite ("and revealed here for the first time") in his "Five S Formula": Stop 'em/Show 'em/Seduce 'em/Satisfy 'em/Sell 'em.

Stop 'em: with a headline to separate prospects from everyone else.

Show 'em: words and no words: pictures, people, images, all reinforcing the headline.

Seduce 'em: emotional needs, fantasy, self-image.

Sell 'em: Ask for the order. (See AFTO under Considine.)

PIERRE PASSAVANT
Passavant Seminars & Consulting

It's not *exactly* a formula, says international lecturer and consultant Passavant, but it works! He calls it the Escalator of Promotion Intensity (EPI). His point: There is a difference between "ordinary" and "extraordinary" offers. "That difference," says Pierre, "is often in the intensity of the promotional elements used. The more the intensity, the higher the response potential." And then adds, cautiously, "most of the time. . . ."

JERRY REITMAN
Vice President, Leo Burnett

It was Henry Hoke who gave this advice for newcomers in direct mail copywriting: "Blue pencil the first paragraph." His point: It usually takes a new writer that long to get to the point. He felt beginners tended to approach a sales proposition with the bullpen aproach, taking a few paragraphs to warm up.

Jerry Reitman says almost the same thing with this WIDDWO formula. Translation: *When In Doubt, Do Without.*"

One more from Jerry: QTBP = *Quality Is The Best Policy.*

JAMES ROSENFIELD
President, Buchanan/Vinson/Rosenfield Direct

Rosenfield gave a series of DM seminars across the country with John Booth, Senior VP of the Direct Marketing Group. John writes, "Our seminar registrants were convinced Jim's METHOD is the definitive Formula to End all DM Formulas."

Jim's METHOD reads from top to bottom:

*M*otivate
*E*lucidate
*T*angibilize
*H*umanize
*O*ver-simplify
*D*irect!

Why not? If METHOD works for Actor's Studio graduates, why not for Jim Rosenfield?

JOE SUGARMAN
JS&A Sales

"My formula is called the 'Slippery Slide' Theory," says top copywriter Sugarman. (See R I C on page 22)

"Simply stated, if you climb on a slide that is slippery, you are going to slide all the way to the bottom unable to stop. That's the way I do my ads. Once you start reading them, you can't stop. Then, if you're a good salesman, you're going to get your message across on the ride down."

Joe also built his famous seminars around this basic theory.

JOHN FRANCIS TIGHE
(One of Direct Marketing's top free-lance copywriters)

"The nation's second best copywriter," (as he calls himself) comes in with his own solution aptly labeled, "Tighe's 3 M's."

1. Merchandise the offer.
2. Multiply the benefits.
3. Massage the prospect.

WALTER SCHMID
International Direct Marketing Symposium

The Master Entrepreneur of them all writes us from his mini-castle in Zurich, Switzerland. He has seen the world's experts perform for nearly twenty years on his international stage in Montreux.

After hearing and seeing them all, he simply says, "I think your list is complete."

He adds, "Should I run across another formula, I would let you know." We're going to write Walter back and say Don't tell us. This is it. No more. As Carlyle said, "It is now almost my sole rule of life to cleanse myself of all formulas."

3
Give Me Five!
(Or, The Five Ways
Advertising Works)

THE PATIENT WAKES UP in the hospital room after the operation.
He does *not* say, *"How* am I?" He does say, *"Where* am I?" He wants to be in control, which starts with being in a *familiar* environment.

Being familiar is a basic need and one of the five ways advertising works.

All five were first discussed more than twenty years ago by James Webb Young, a director of J. Walter Thompson and recognized by many as the dean of American advertising.

Here's a checklist to match against *your* advertising. Does it meet one (or more) of these five rules?

1. **Be familiar.**
2. **Be a reminder.**
3. **Be newsworthy.**
3. **Be action-stimulating.**
5. **Be added value.**

Let's examine them one by one to see how they work for you in putting together your next direct mail campaign.

1. Be Familiar. Ever drive down a strange road at nighttime? Notice how much longer it seems than in . . . daytime? Reason: it is simply not "familiar" to you.

People *want* to be in a familiar setting. And/or buy a familiar product. Once buying-habit patterns are set, they are difficult to change. Friends like to take you to a restaurant *they* enjoy, to see you buy a car *they* appreciate, to have you purchase a book *they* read. They are comfortable because their choices are familiar to them.

When you go shopping you reach for the "familiar" brands because you used them before, or you saw the name in an ad. That is the reason no-name generic food advertising makes up only a tiny fraction of the food business. The recognition of savings in dollars is not strong enough to overcome the lack of recognition.

Psychologists call this a "degree of comfort." Your customers do not have to make a new decision on whether or not the purchase serves their needs. It did before. It will again. They are *comfortable* making the decision to buy.

What does this have to do with your mailing to your customer?

This: *you passed the first test.* Because your customers *are* familiar with you. They will open up *and read* what you mailed them.

A recent readership survey revealed twice as many people who own a product had read an advertisement of the product as those who never bought the product.

Familiarity. It works. To bring the customer *in*.

2. *Be a Reminder.* Look at the calendar. Every month except August has at least one holiday. Most are reasons for buying . . . something. Valentine's Day. Halloween. Christmas. Mother's and Father's and Grandmother's and Grandfather's and Secretary's Day. Industries lobby for the Mayor or Governor or President to proclaim a "day" for their individual industry. Reason: to encourage people to buy for that holiday. Once you set a habit pattern, it is difficult to stop. Think about it: Fish on Fridays. Hot cross buns for Easter.

The raisin industry wanted to increase sales of their product. They promoted, "Fresh raisin bread on Wednesday." It worked.

Our largest single business day is on New Year's Day. We promote this first day of our fall and winter sale *only* by direct mail. No radio. No newspaper. No TV. Nothing except direct mail. People know when it will happen and have appeared regularly *for the past twenty years!* All we do is *remind* them.

And how about political parties? A few weeks before the election you are *reminded* to vote and *how* to vote.

And your church gives or sends you a bulletin to tell you what is happening at services this week and to *remind* you of other church activities.

Shoe stores send out notes every few months to *remind* you it is time to come in for a new pair of shoes for your children's growing feet.

Optometrists and dentists *remind* you it's check-up time.

Joe Girard (America's #1 Automobile salesman) spent more than $25,000 a year on postcards to his customers. Once every month. To *remind* them of the holiday that month and also that he was still around selling the same merchandise in the same place at the same address.

January: "Happy New Year. I like you. Joe Girard."
February: 'Happy Valentine's Day. I like you. Joe Girard."
March: "Happy St. Ptarick's Day. I like you. Joe Girard."

One card a month to celebrate a holiday and remind you he was thinking of you. And an extra one on your birthday—"your special day." Think about it, next time you buy a car. Will you buy one from someone who likes you?

Reminding. It works. To bring the customer back.

3. Be newsworthy. This is how public relations people make their money. They come up with ideas that make the *news* columns instead of the *advertising* columns.

If your direct mailer is *newsworthy* to your customer, they will come to see . . . and buy.

The arrival of the personal computer was news. And each subsequent addition, edition and improvement is news. And sells computers.

Notice how many times you see the word "new" atop soap powder and cereals. Because "new" *is* "news."

Reese Palley, self-styled "Merchant to the Rich" art dealer in Atlantic City decided to celebrate his fiftieth birthday with his customers. Their obligation: Buy a Dali lithograph. Their reward: a free round-trip weekend in Paris. His direct mail piece went to a few thousand customers. Cost five cents each. Results: He sold out two 747s—the *only* individual to ever pull that off. His profit: In the millions. The publicity—front pages on newspapers and magazines throughout the world. Now, *that's* newsworthy.

You can create your own news by opening a new department in your store:

• Creating early opening or late opening hours.

• Running a special promotion and/or sale you want your regular customers to knew about before anyone else.

• Introducing a *new* product to your customer.

Newsworthy. It works. To bring the customers *reasons to buy.*

4. Be action stimulating. A mail order color page in *Life* magazine received a Starch "most read" rating of 20 percent. But . . . the response in orders was only 1/10th of one percent of the circulation.

What happened? People read the ad. But only a small percentage "acted" on the ad.

The bottom line of good advertising is not how many awards are won by the agency but how much money is spent by the customer. Salesmen know this. The "close" of the sale is the most important part. It is fine to have a marvelous introduction. It is commendable to have a package of reasons why people should buy. Both mean nothing if no sale takes place.

Salesmen are taught to remember the ABC's of selling: *A*lways *B*e *C*losing. They are reminded by their sales managers over and over again to AFTO— Ask For The Order.

Direct marketing people agree. They tell you to ask for the order *within* the ad. *In* the order blank. *On* the envelope. They tell the customer what they have to do in order to buy, purchase, receive the merchandise. Tell the reader to "write your name and address here" or "cut along this line." Or "take off the yes (or no) peel-off label and put it here."

This is called *involvement*. The more you are successful in involving your readers in doing . . . *something* with your mailer, the greater the odds they will buy. (See Rule 5, page 17)

How do you motivate the reader to pick up the pencil and fill in her name, address and credit card number?

The desire to act is already there simmering down deep inside the consumer. Your mailer must make it explode into action.

• Everyone wants to have money for retirement. Now where do they put the money? In the bank? The insurance company? The stock market?

• Everyone has to buy food and clothing. Now, how do you have them come to your food store. Or clothing store?

Sometimes the right *word* will work. They do not sell life insurance in England or Australia. They sell life *assurance*. That has a different sound. If insurance means they pay off when I leave, does assurance mean I'm going to be around a while longer?

The insurance company that offers *life* benefits intrigues me far more than the one that offers me *death* benefits. How does *death* benefit me?

We once attended a meeting with some business people. We asked what their plans were for that day.

The real estate man said he was going to show some houses. The insurance man said he was going to line up some physicals for customers. The clothing man said he was going to show some clothes. The manufacturer's rep said he would show some new products to prospects. The banker said he would wind up that week's officer call program.

But not one said . . . "I'm going to make a sale."

Be action stimulating. It works. To bring reasons *why* the customer should act.

5.   *Be added value*. See those open boxes of baking soda in refrigerators all over America making the refrigerators smell nicer! But, uh . . . isn't baking soda supposed to be used for baking?

Sure. But the company came up with *another and additional reason to buy the product*. They practiced line-extension. If you own a major share of the market with what you make, how can you add a *new* market?

Shake 'n Bake advertises the product as a base for a pie as well as a coating for chicken.

L'Eggs mails to nurses catalogs offering only white pantyhose.

Hershey chocolate markets chocolate milk in a cardboard container that looks just like the candy bar.

Gerber baby food adds its name and reputation to baby clothing and accessories.

Added value can also be prestige. The perception is more important than the actuality.

The "CM" for Countess Mara on your tie. The package from Tiffany's. The Avanti car, Movado watch, Steuben glass, Rosenthal China, Ralph Lauren's Polo Player . . .

Added value. It works. To bring an extra reason why the customer will buy from you.

Use one or more of these five reasons why advertising works in your next mailer and you automatically increase the odds for your success.

TOOLBOX

"Send me a ~~man~~ *PERSON* who *reads!*"

In the early 1960s the International Paper Company ran a series of advertisements with the theme (and the headline), "Send me a man who *reads!*" Today they would have to change this to "Send me a *person* who reads." But the message remains the same; successful people are readers. In extensive research, International Paper studied the reading habits of 100 young businessmen who were members of management training programs and considered likely to become executives.

They found that these men read an average of three magazines and 12 newspapers a week . . .

An identical survey among 100 company vice presidents between the ages of 45 and 50 found that, in a single week, these busy men found time to read an average of three and a half magazines and 15 newspapers.

Similar studies show successful architects, teachers, scientists, salespeople, politicians read more than their less successful counterparts.

The point International Paper emphasized in every ad was that people keep on reading as their careers move upward.

In the realm of direct mail, (particularly do-it-yourself direct mail), we feel reading trade publications and books on direct mail, and above all, reading other people's direct mail, is a key to real success in your own mail efforts.

With the reading of *The Do-It-Yourself Direct Mail Handbook* you're off to a good start. But you can't stop there. Our book is designed to give you the basics, the ability to produce result-getting direct mail pieces for your business or profession to get you started.

Direct mail, however, is fast moving. There are new techniques in production, changed postal regulations, advanced concepts in copy and design, significant differences in test results and many other variables that will help you improve your direct mail.

Similarly, once involved in direct mail, you will want to go beyond the basics. You will find much of the help you need in the many excellent books available on direct mail and direct marketing.

Our *Toolbox* for this chapter lists books and periodicals that should be in your library and on your subscription list. The total cost of both the books and periodicals will not exceed the price of a good seminar on the subject.

In the future, when the success comes that will be yours through direct mail, part of the reason will be because you designed and wrote your mailing pieces as someone who . . . reads!

And here are some books to start with . . .

Elements of Direct Marketing, by Martin Baier. ($34.95)

Baier uniquely combines the best of both theory and practice as they apply to direct marketing. This book thoroughly demonstrates the close interaction of direct marketing with finance, production, economics and contemporary scientific disciplines. Each chapter concludes with a state-of-the-art case history of direct marketing at work.

Successful Direct Marketing Methods, 2nd Edition, by Bob Stone. ($27.95)

This book is called the Bible of direct marketing. The entire scope of direct response techniques are fully explained in a practical, down-to-earth style that covers examples and case histories of actual companies, plus nearly 100 illustrations of effective ads. 370 pages.

Profitable Direct Marketing, by Jim Kobs. ($24.95)

How to start, improve or expand any direct marketing operation. Includes 11 detailed case studies of prominent direct marketing companies.

Ogilvy on Advertising, by David Ogilvy. ($24.95)

This book is as witty and outspoken as the man who wrote it. It will make profitable reading for everyone whose job is to sell a product, a corporation, or a policy. Reveals everything Ogilvy has learned about which advertising techniques sell and which don't sell. Illustrated with 185 advertisements (many in full color).

Common Sense Direct Marketing, by Drayton Bird. ($26.00)

For newcomer and experienced marketer alike, this lively new book utilizes a very different approach from one of England's most talented writers and direct mail agency head. "The one book you'll actually enjoy, the perfect mixture of the practical and amusing." 208 pages.

Direct Mail and Mail Order Handbook, 3rd Edition, by Richard S. Hodgson. ($57.50)

Points the way to success in every element of direct mail advertising and mail order selling. You can plan, create and produce the most complicated direct mail campaigns down to the last detail with absolute confidence. Provides proven ideas reliable reference data and checklists which ensure success for your mail campaign. 1,555 pages.

Tested Advertising Methods, 4th Edition, by John Caples. ($14.95)
For over three decades this book has been the standard guide on tested methods of getting favorable sales results from advertising. What headlines attract readers; 29 formulas for writing headlines; how to write the first paragraph; how to make small ads pay big; 32 ways to get more inquiries; 20 ways to increase selling power; 17 ways to test your ads . . . plus more! 318 pages.

The Basics of Copy, by Ed McLean. ($15.00)
Practical, money-saving information on how to use copy to structure the appeal of the product or service to the mailing list. Paperback. 132 pages.

But Would Saks Fifth Avenue Do It?, by Murray Raphel. ($10.00)
A collection of Murray Raphel's best "Ideas For Retailers" columns from *Direct Marketing Magazine* (1961–1981). Hundreds of ideas for you and your business. More than a book on direct mail, a masterpiece on how to think creatively, how to motivate, how to sell, how to practice salesmanship in print. Paperback. 128 pages.

Mail Order Magic, by Herman Poltz. ($15.95)
In clear, concise style, this book shows how the proven techniques of direct mail can help generate greater sales and profits in business outside of catalog and other conventional mail order marketing. Among the subjects: making sales vs. making customers, how to write inquiry advertising, costs of doing business, basic rules of testing, analyzing and evaluating results, the great white space myth, and how to generate lists.

The Great Brain Robbery, by Ray Considine and Murray Raphel. ($15.00)
Two of direct mail's great champions present a collection of proven ideas to make you money and change your life! Over 2,000 borrowable ideas in words and pictures reveal the authors' super secrets of selling, merchandising and marketing for you and your business. 221 pages.

How to Make Your Advertising Twice as Effective at Half the Cost, by Herschell Gordon Lewis. ($8.95)
This "advertising survival kit" is a practical guide written for anyone trying to unscramble the confusion in the ad world and create advertising

for his own business, aimed at the small- and medium-sized business not blessed with a large advertising budget. Paperback. 207 pages.

Handbook of Business Letters, by Roy W. Poe. ($35.95)
Focusing on the need of letter writers in all kinds of businesses, this book examines more than 160 different letter-writing situations—and provides model letters to demonstrate how each of these diverse situations can be handled effectively. 286 pages.

If any of these books are of interest to you, write:

THE MARKETERS BOOKSHELF
402 Bethlehem Pike
Philadelphia, PA 19118

OR . . .

DIRECT MARKETING
224 Seventh Street
Garden City, NY 11530

OR . . .

DIRECT MARKETING ASSOCIATION
6 East 43rd Street
New York, NY 10017

PART TWO:
PRODUCING THE PACKAGE

4

I'm Going to Make You
an Offer You Can't Refuse

- How to put your commercial on station WII-FM.
- The basic rule in selling . . . and how it works.
- The one person responsible for your business's success.
- Everything depends on the proper point of view.

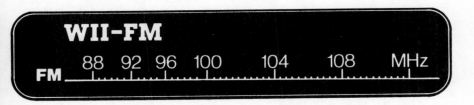

"WE'RE GOING TO PLAY a fun game tonight," said the hostess as the guests arrived.

After dinner she explained the game.

Each person would have someone's name taped to his or her back. They would then ask anyone in the room questions about this "person." Each had ten minutes to guess the name of their mystery person.

The famous ones were easy. The movie stars took only a few minutes. But half-way through the evening, one person simply could not guess the name on his back. He asked all the right questions and finally, at the ten minute limit, gave up.

"Don't you really have any idea who the person could be?" asked the hostess.

"No," he replied. "None of the descriptions or answers seemed in the least bit familiar."

The hostess took off the name and showed it to him.

It was his own.

What happened?

This: Each of us has an image of who we are to ourselves that does not necessarily correspond to who we are to others.

This point of view is very important to remember in direct mail. For if we are marketing directly to an individual (and we are), we must understand their point of view *before* we write any words.

Remember, every one of your potential customers is listening to an FM radio station in his home. The call letters are WII-FM.

This station has a clear channel and broadcasts across the entire world. Your customers listen to this station twenty-four hours a day. Consciously while they are awake. Subconsciously while they are sleeping. Your job, as an advertiser, is to put your commercial on this station.

Oh, by the way, the initials WII-FM stand for *What's In It For Me?*

The customer knows what's in it for *you*. He spends *his* money in *your* place of business. But . . . what's in it for *him?* Why should he shop with you or buy your services instead of your competition's? What are you doing to make your offer more attractive, unusual . . . profitable?

To answer that question, you have to know there is really one basic rule to success in selling. Here it is. You never have to attend any more selling seminars or read any more books. Just memorize this one sentence, follow what it says and your success is assured: FIND OUT WHAT YOUR CUSTOMERS WANT AND GIVE IT TO THEM.

Now reprint that phrase and put it on the wall in front of your desk where you can read it before you start your next direct mail campaign.

Let's stop for a minute so we're all sure we're talking about the same thing.

What we are *not* talking about in this chapter is what you have to sell. We are *not* talking about your bank's Certificate of Deposit, your store's clothing, your professional service, your new, just-arrived item in the warehouse.

Those are products or services.

What we *are* talking about is how to sell those products or services.

That's what we mean by offer. What do you *offer* the customer so he *wants* to buy? Your offer is the way you present your product or service, the benefits and the price in terms of the reader's desires, needs, wants, dreams. Now, your offer has to be what the customer wants to buy. Not wht you think she wants to buy.

How do you find out?

Remember the fellow at the party who didn't know it was his name on his back? Try that for starters. What is your customer's point of view?

Some tire salesmen feel they should tell customers how steel belted tires are made with seven cords of steel wrapped together to form strong reinforcement. But we want to hear how safe the tires are when our spouse drives the children to school.

Travel agents do not sell the time payments needed to buy the airline tickets. They sell romance, glamour, excitement.

Clothing salesmen do not sell stitches to the inch. They sell fashion, style, appeal to the opposite sex.

We all know businesspeople who say, "I'm going to buy what I like for my store. If the customer doesn't like it, too bad."

Well, too bad for those businesspeople. They soon fold up their retailing tent and wonder where they went wrong.

This does not mean your individual taste and selection and choice does not enter into what you sell. Of course it does.

What it does mean: After establishing certain parameters, guidelines and choices, how do you find out what your customer wants to buy? People's taste and style and choice of what they want to eat, wear, watch, read or participate in continually changes. In some cases gradually. In some, overnight.

Somewhere in this promised land there are warehouses full of men's Nehru shirts and women's satin hot pants and hula hoops and blotters waiting for that style to return. Someday. Maybe. Great ideas whose time came . . . and went. We can be sure the only thing that remains constant . . . is change.

As a businessperson, how do you know—really *know*—what product or service your customer wants to buy?

One way is to test. And this way is available to you in only *one* form of advertising: direct mail.

When a piece of merchandise or service sells well, the buyer is quick to be recognized as the one who made the decision and quick to claim the credit and wear the laurel wreath.

When a piece of merchandise does not sell well, it is the fault of the manufacturer ("He changed it from when I bought it"), the salesman ("He is very high pressure, you know") or the timing (We're just ahead of everybody else. They need a chance to catch up.")

It is indeed true that victory has many parents and defeat is an orphan.

We can narrow the defeats, increase the wins and be thought of as the person to hire, the store to shop or the business on the move if we simply test what we want to offer the public before we make major commitments. Department stores do this all the time. They strike fear in the hearts of suppliers with, "We'll try a few dozen. If it clicks, we expect you to fill all our orders at once." Great for department stores. Disaster for small businesses that do not have the clout or impact to back up these demands.

When you have a new product or service, instead of sending out your next mailing piece to your entire mailing list, why not simply "test" it with a percentage of your mailing list? A very, very small percentage of your list will show you what the probable results would be if you mail the entire list. (More on testing in Chapter 16).

Testing is extremely valuable to you if you really believe in your product and feel it offers a benefit to your customer. Your first mailing may not be profitable. This does not necessarily mean the offer you made is bad. It may mean the *approach* you made is not working. People who use direct mail and claim they are merely advertising products to fill their customer's "needs" are living in the wrong century. We have not been a "needy" country for more than fifty years. Today's successful businesses are not need-fillers. They are want-creators.

As little children we are asked by adults, "What do you want to be when you grow up?" No one says, "What do you *need* to be?"

The reason is simple. If you "want" something strongly enough, you will produce it, work for it or buy it.

Our job, as salespeople, is to create *wants*. One way we can do this is by listening to our customers. All of us in selling are usually so concerned with getting across a message of what we want to sell we don't take the time to listen to what the customer wants to buy.

Your customers care. They want to know. They will respond to your calling or writing as long as you can make an offer to them of something they want.

Too many small businesses forget about the customers who feel the business forgot about them.

What does *that* mean?

In a recent survey on why customers do not shop a business they once shopped, this was the percentage return:
- 68 percent had no special reason;
- 15 percent had complaints that were not taken care of properly;
- 9 percent were lured away by other businesses (better service or lower prices);
- 9 percent moved.

In other words: nearly 7 out of 10 good customers leave because your business lets them leave.

You plan and work out your direct mailers to bring customers into your store. But what are you doing to keep them coming back?

Harry Bullis of General Mills told a convention of Northwestern Life 'Insurance representatives: "When I go out in the morning I don't ask 'How many sales will I make today?' I ask, 'How many people can I help today?'"

The small businessman knows his customer better than anyone else.

He can quote the German proverb, "Ich Kenne mein Volk," which means, "I know my people." This personal relationship is your strongest selling tool.

The Psychology of the Second Interest

Remember we said making the sales was simply finding out what the customer wanted to buy and give it to him? At this point you might well ask, "What if what *I* have to sell is not what *they* want to buy?"

Good question. And time to try a selling technique we call, "The Psychology of the Second Interest." Here's what it means:

You can have someone buy something you want to *sell them if you offer them something else they* want to *buy.*

Go back and read that sentence one more time.

Here's an example: Do you buy Crackerjacks for the carmel popcorn . . . or the prize?

Do you buy a new fragrance for the fragrance or for the free umbrella or low cost baggage that is yours with every purchase? Do you subscribe to magazines for the magazine or the chance to win $100,000 a year for life? Or a new home? Or a new car?

Do you go to conventions to go to conventions or because it's a tax-deductible reason to visit San Francisco?

Take a look at breakfast cereal boxes in your kitchen cabinet. Post Grape Nuts recently offered a chance to win "free athletic equipment for your school" by saving the seals on the side of the cereal box. Del Monte raisins offered you a $15 embossed hardcover world atlas (300 pages, 190 in full color) for half price if you sent in the label to the box.

If this doesn't work (it usually does) then you can fall back upon the TOOOLBOX section that follows, which we call: *The Psychology of Many Options.*

TOOLBOX

The more ways you offer your customer to buy from you in the mail, the greater your response.

- *Ways to pay.* If the product must be bought with cash, you eliminate a lot of buyers. Each new way you give them to purchase your product, you increase sales: Credit cards. C.O.D.'s, time payments, 30-day charges, checks . . .
- *Special price offers.* The item can be bought for a reduced price but only for a specified length of time. Give the exact date and hold to it.
- *Discount for quantity.* If you buy now, the price is so much less. And if you buy five it's even less.
- *Timing.* It can be done by picking the right time and right place. This greatly increasese sales of the right product or service.
- *Free information.* Even if they do *not* buy the product, have them respond to some brochure, booklet, newsletter, something you give them free for simply checking the appropriate box.
- *Free gift.* You've all seen this one. If you order the item, you also receive, free of charge, this special . . . something. And you keep the something whether or not you decide to keep the item ordered. (It is not unusual to have a free gift increase your orders by at least 25 percent!) But select a gift suited to *personal* use. It will have far more appeal.
- *Not if but which.* Always give your customer a choice between something and something, not something and nothing. We succeed in selling clothing because we always ask the customer to make a decision *between* items, never a yes/no decision:

"Do you like white or pastel shirts?"
"Do you like striped or solid ties?"
"Do you like button down or plain collar shirts?" Make the same offer in your mailing. Give the customer a choice. Ask them *which* they prefer. And last, but not least . . . *THE GUARANTEE.*

GUARANTEE

In 1861, the Austrian foreign minister, Johann Berhnard Graf
Von Rechberg was asked to comment upon papers recently drawn with
guarantees concerning the recognition of Italy. His comment,
"Guarantees are not worth the paper they are written on."

True in 1861. Not true today. Especially with the Federal Trade
Commission watching.

Guarantees inspire confidence. Nearly 100 years ago, Sears Roebuck
guaranteed satisfaction for everything in their catalogue. Nearly
half a century ago Good Housekeeping made the word famous with
their "satisfaction guaranteed or replacement of merchandise."

THROUGH THE YEARS, NO ONE HAS SUCCEEDED IN MAIL ORDER WITHOUT OFFERING
THE CONSUMER A GUARANTEE.

Norm Thompson in Portland, Oregon copyrighted their "You be the Judge"
guarantee. They guarantee their merchandise for the normal life of
the product, "you being the judge of what that normal life should be."

Publix supermarkets in Florida advertise their food is guaranteed
until you have enjoyed every morsel. When the senior citizens were
asked why they shopped Publix some answered, "Because they guarantee
their food." It was pointed out to them all supermarkets guarantee
their food. "Really?" said the skeptical ones, "how come they don't
say so?" (Which is why Publix owns 25% of every food dollar spent
in Florida.

Guarantee your merchandise you sell! Do not assume your customer
knows you do. Tell them. And don't make exceptions.

Make it simple to read and understand. L. L. Bean in Maine simply
says, "Our products are guaranteed to be 100% satisfactory. Return
anything purchased from us that proves otherwise. We will replace
it or refund your money as you wish."

Spencer Gifts, one of the nation's leading mail catalogue companies
simply says on top of their order blank: "Satisfaction guaranteed
or your money refunded." Only six words. But it says it all.

Guarantees reinforce the confidence the customer has with you...
with your merchandise.

SATISFACTION GUARANTEED OR YOUR MONEY BACK

Any teacher or good student of direct mail will tell you how important a guarantee is when selling your merchandise through the mail. It gives you an added advantage because the customer now has confidence he can trust you.

If a customer brought defective merchandise back to you—or was even simply dissatisfied with your product—would you try to make the customer happy? Would you offer a refund or a replacement of money? If you wanted to see that customer again, you would. That is why the overwhelming number of catalogs and products sold through the mail highlight their guarantee. They want to *make sure* their customer is satisfied.

Well, with one notable exception: many department stores. Those established institutions of retailing throughout the country send many pieces through the mail offering goods and services for sale. But rarely do they offer the same guarantee printed in the catalogue that you find from a competitive company doing most of their business through the mail and often times selling the exact same product as the department store.

Why do so many stores and businesses leave out the guarantee in their mailings even though, in reality they do "guarantee" what they sell?

Here's what some answered: "Those catalogs go to our customers. They know who we are. They know we will guarantee everything we sell."

Do they?

And aren't the other folks sending out catalogues sending them to *their* customers? And yet they repeat the guarantee in every issue.

Do you think someone should tell some of those that take the customer for granted about the Curse of Assumption?

L. L. Bean Guarantee

It began with a waterproof shoe to go duck hunting. And now this Maine retailer does more than $250 million a year selling merchandise through the mail. And his guarantee has not changed through the years because . . . it works.

> ### 100% Guarantee
> All of our products are guaranteed to give 100% satisfaction in every way. Return anything purchased from us at any time if it proves otherwise. We will replace it, refund your purchase price or credit your credit card, as you wish. We do not want you to have anything from L.L. Bean that is not completely satisfactory.

Eddie Bauer Guarantee

Known originally for selling warm jackets, this mail marketeer is known for his quality merchandise and his very, very simple guarantee that literally tells you like it is.

OUR GUARANTEE

Every item we sell will give complete satisfaction or you may return it for a full refund.

Shoreham Clothing

We like this one because they call it the "famous" Shoreham Guarantee. And say *you* must be satisfied or you receive a refund, a credit or a replacement. *Your* choice.

THE FAMOUS SHOREHAM GUARANTEE.

The quality and workmanship of the merchandise in this catalog is **unconditionally guaranteed** by Shoreham. Should you be dissatisfied for any reason, with the fit, style or wear of your purchase, we urge you to return it for replacement or a full refund, or credit to your card account if you prefer.

The Sharper Image Guarantee

Clearly spelled out to (1) give you thirty days to make up your mind (2) say their price is the lowest and (3) have a one-year quality guarantee.

Three reasons why you enjoy shopping more with The Sharper Image.

1. You have 30 days to make up your mind.
If not satisfied, simply return the item (in new condition, please) within 30 days for a prompt, courteous refund, whatever the reason. Your satisfaction is the only judge.

2. You get the best value. We match any advertised price.
You won't see the same item advertised for less elsewhere. If you do; just send us the advertisement within 30 days of receiving the item. We'll refund or credit the difference to you.

3. You own a durable, well-made product, with a one-year quality guarantee.
We make sure every product is backed by a reputable manufacturer's service center. If you don't get prompt satisfactory service, in or out of warranty, call our Customer Relations representatives. Use the toll free Customer Relations number—800-344-5555. We'll make sure your item is fixed or replaced in a reasonable time, or your money will be refunded—up to a full year after purchase.

The Omaha Fixture Guarantee

They put it in capital letters and bold face so you could not miss the message: *NO TIME LIMIT. NO SMALL PRINT.*

OUR GUARANTEE TO YOU

All racks manufactured by Omaha Fixture are guaranteed to be free of defects, in both material and workmanship.

**NO TIME LIMIT
NO SMALL PRINT**

Will your *PRESENT* RACK SUPPLIER put *THAT* in writing?

Norm Thompson Guarantee

This is our favorite. Not only because they have *trademarked* their guarantee but also because they spell it out in very explicit terms telling you it is *not* a 2-week guarantee but "good for the normal life of the product" and the clincher line, "You being the judge of what the normal life should be . . ."

"You be the Judge™" Guarantee

When we say "You be the Judge™," we mean just that! Every product you purchase from Norm Thompson must live up to YOUR expectations, not ours. If at any time a product fails to satisfy you, return it to us, postage prepaid, and we'll either replace the item, or refund your money in full, whichever you wish.

This is definitely not a 2-week guarantee. It's good for the normal life of the product. (You being the judge of what that normal life should be.) We'll stand behind everything we sell to the fullest extent...no if's, and's or but's.

5
Take Our Word for It

"When I used a word," Humpty Dumpty said in rather a scornful tone, "it means just what I choose it to mean—neither more nor less."

"The question is," said Alice, "whether you can make the words mean so many different things."

"The question is," said Humpty Dumpty, "which is to be master —that's all."

—Alice in Wonderland

"Do you know why Confucius said, 'A picture is worth a thousand words'?"

The speaker was Vrest Orton. We were chatting with him in Weston, Vermont, home of his Original Vermont Country Store. There on the walls are autographed photographs of presidents past: (Eisenhower, Truman, (Coolidge.) Poets past: (Robert Frost.) and prosers past who gave him their first editions because he is also a writer: Sinclair, Parker, Benchley.

Vrest believes words communicate. His "Voice of the Mountains" catalog is 80 percent words, only 20 percent pictures. The exact reverse of today's four color photo-dominated catalogues. He believes that, in the beginning, there was the word.

"Do you know why Confucius said, 'A picture is worth a thousand words'?" he repeated.

Well, we thought perhaps because a picture would graphically sum up a story, or show a product, or convey a mood or image or . . .

"Wrong!" said Vrest. And then he told us his theory.

"In the time of Confucius, very few Chinese could read. But they could understand pictures. And so a picture *was* worth a thousand words— because very few people could read the words. But they could *see* the pictures."

The success of Orton's catalog shows his belief in the success of words to convey selling messages better than pictures. Orton says, "Our catalog is for people who can read. If you can't read, we don't send it to you . . ."*

Those who put paper into the typewriter (or speed along on their word processor) know what words can do: convey every emotional expression and in many different ways. They can take a long time to make their point. Or make it quick. Short. Sudden.

In Ed Mayer's book, *How to Make More Money with Your Direct Mail* published nearly *forty* years ago, he mentioned writer H. Phelps Gates telling readers of the *Christian Science Monitor* about the effect of words on readers. He listed the strength and force in short words: blast, boom, throb, thump, clank, chime, hiss, buzz. He then mentioned words you can "hear" like the swish of silk. Words that convey a sense of smell like musk and cheese and mint and rose. All those words tell us something.

It does get confusing sometimes, however, when we find ourselves overwhelmed with oxymorons. These are the two-word phrases where the second word cancels out the first.

Example: A recent quote from the Prime Minister of Israel who said, "My job is to worry about the *future history* of Israel." Difficult to be both future *and* history.

Jumbo shrimp. (How can it be jumbo if it's also shrimp?)

Plastic glasses. (How can it be plastic if it is also glass?)

And then there's military intelligence and congressional ethics. (How can it be military if it's also, . . . well, you get the idea.)

How about the TV shows advertised as "epic mini-series." And we are really confused about a recent automobile ad that offered me "mandatory options."

If words preceding (or following) words are not enough to confuse your reader, don't forget those little friends "prefix" and "suffix" that hang around in front of or back of a word and—presto—the word takes on a *new* meaning.

When a lawyer is removed from his job, he is disbarred. And a priest is defrocked. Now, our question today, students, is do electricians become delighted, musicians denoted, cowboys deranged, models deposed and judges distorted?

Does a baker become unrolled, a teacher degraded, a songwriter decomposed, a podiatrist defeated, a detective dissolved and a florist deflowered? (Is an ex-pot smoker disjointed?)

And so, folks, there is the constant challenge to find out the way to write and the words to use that are best understood by your readers. One good rule: The words that worked before will continue to work in the

---

*Vrest is one of those rare writers who could also write good advertising copy. Among those who tried and failed: Charles Lamb, Byron, Bernard Shaw, Hemingway, Marquand, Sherwood Anderson.

future. Winston Churchill said, "the short words are the best and the old words best of all."

Napoleon said, "It is astonishing what power words can have over man." (Can we have a show of hands from those who agree with this? . . . Good!) All the more reason to choose the *right* word. Sometimes difficult because . . . the same word can have different meanings. There are more than 14,000 meanings for the 500 most commonly used words in the English language!

Pity the stranger trying to learn English who finds the word pronounced "plane."

Now he must determine if this word means a vehicle that flies, or an ordinary looking person, a flatness of terrain or a carpenter's tool.

Then there is the problem of words spelled in such a way you would think they would rhyme. But they don't. Like: freak and break. Sew and few. Horse and worse. Beard and heard. Cord and word. Cow and low. Shoe and foe. Goose and choose. Nose and dose. And you think English is an *easy* language to understand?

(No wonder the Chinese said, "Where's the pictures?")

Copy: The Long & Short of It

How long should your copy be?

There is the short school and the long school.

The short school include the ones who insist all memos must be on one page. Preferably double spaced.

The long school says to write all the information you have in your mailing.

The correct answer is to write until you finish what you want to say. People will keep on reading as long as it is interesting for them to keep on reading. (Read that last sentence one more time.)

Our favorite long *vs.* short copy is the landlord who decided to evict his tenants. His lawyer sent all the residents a thick, legal long-copy document listing all the reasons they had to move.

One tenant responded with this classic short-style copy:

Dear Sir,
I remain
Very truly yours.

Every one of your mailing pieces is a complete sales pitch for your product. Sometimes you can say it all in five words. Sometimes it takes five hundred.

But as long as it is interesting to read, the reader will read.

Many studies show readership falls off quickly up to the first 50 words. But if they read the first 50, they will read the next 500.

Boyce Morgan, the writer responsible for many of the early direct mail successes of the *Kiplinger Letter* once conducted tests on long *vs.* short copy. His results: when you cut copy down to simply fit on *one* sheet of paper you also cut down on orders.

The "more you tell, the more you sell" school of writing is championed by Dr. Charles Edwards of the graduate school of retailing at New York University. He says, "The more facts you tell, the more you sell. An advertisement's chance for success increases as the number of pertinent merchandise facts indicated in the advertisement increases."

Think about that for a minute.

Each of you has received a thick pack of executive cards in the mail, each representing a different product. Readership of this mailing is much higher than if each item was mailed one by one.

Have you received a packet of coupons from the local supermarket recently? They do not mail you one coupon for one item but rather many coupons for many items. Their theory: you will want *one* of the many.

Famous advertising writer Claude Hopkins once wrote five pages of copy to promote Schlitz beer. Schlitz's sales moved it from fifth place to first place in a short time.

Writer Vic Schwab tells the story of Max Hart (of Hart, Schaffner & Marx). Hart disliked long copy. He continually rejected ads with too many words. One day his advertising manager said, "I'll bet you ten dollars I can write a newspaper ad of copy and you will read every word. And you will agree if I just show you just the headline."

Hart took the bet, read the headline and said, "OK, you win. Run the ad."

This was the headline: "This ad is all about Max Hart."

Does Your Writing Sound Like You Talking?

Every expert you talk to on direct mail will tell you to "write as you talk." Which is fine. Up to a point.

If you tape recorded how you sold your product to a customer you would be amazed at how many "Uhhhs" and "ahhhs" and those unforgivable "I," "me" and "ours" that fill out your selling talk.

Yes, of course, it is admirable, effective and to be desired to "write as you talk." But this should be *edited*. Your conversation is chock full of many extra useless words that do not add a single selling point to your effective letter or mailer.

Conversation is also connected with body language that is difficult—if not impossible—to put into your writing. How do you define a twitch of your eye, a shrug of your shoulder, an expressive gesture with your hands—each accompanied by a related phrase.

What "write as you talk" *really* means is that the copy should be smooth and easy to read as good conversation is easy to hear.

Marketing consultant Andrew Byrne, vice-president and creative director of Smith-Hemmings-Gosden, says there are only three deadly failures in advertising:

1. The failure to be simple.
2. The failure to be clear.
3. The failure to be direct.

Each failure can be overcome with short words, short sentences and short paragraphs . . . and the reader will understand what you have to say.

Talk directly to your reader. You know your customer, where he lives, where he works, his problems, hopes, dreams, worries, aspirations, goals. Think *one* customer. Have a clear picture of who he is and what he does.

Now, write to him.

Remember you are really a salesperson behind a typewriter instead of on a selling floor.

Remember your copy is a monologue instead of a dialogue. You are talking to a visualized but unseen audience you must grab and hold and make want to buy.

It is easier if you remember people buy for only one of two reasons. Either your product will give them a new benefit or it will protect a benefit they already have.

Remember the last part of that last sentence. Writers often forget this basic rule: *Fear of loss is greater than promise of gain.*

There is so much emphasis placed on benefits to be gained and worries to be eased and health to be achieved and money to be made, we often overlook an ever stronger attraction: the fear of losing a loved person or possession. (Which is why you see insurance as the number one item sold through the mails in the U.S.—more than $6 billion a year.)

Sometimes you can combine both benefit and protection. Charles Mills of the O.M. Scott Company tells of the millions of dollars they sell in lawn seed, much of it through the mail. Says Mills, "In our copy we must never forget people are interested in their lawn, not in our seeds."

What a powerful selling piece: To those who do *not* have a lawn, here's the way to have a good one. To those who have a good lawn, here's the way to make sure you do not lose it . . ."

If at this point, you're looking for a summary of writing copy, here it is. It works for giving speeches, writing ads, books or plays.

- Say what you are going to say.
- Say it.
- Say what you said.

Start off by telling your reader what you are writing to him about. Explain it. Then summarize what you said.

It's so simple . . . it works.

The finest writers in direct mail write with almost unbelievable simplicity to people with all education levels. For only one reason: It works.

That's why it's called *Direct* mail.

"Then you should say what you mean," the March Hare went on.

"I do," Alice hastily replied; "at least—at least I mean what I say—that's the same thing, you know."

"Not the same thing a bit!" said the Hatter. "Why, you might just as well say that 'I see what I eat' is the same thing as 'I eat what I see'!"

TOOLBOX

Make Sure You Do . . .

1. *Do write an* outline, a guide to follow as you write. Here's one:
   Headline
   First paragraph
   List of benefits
   Proof of benefits
   Reason to buy . . . now!

2. *Do write to a friend . . . enthusiastically.* Don't think of all your customers. Think of one. Write to that one. *And be enthusiastic!* Nothing sells merchandise as much as enthusiasm. Walter Chrysler once said he would pay more for an enthusiastic salesperson than a trained mechanic. And as long as you're writing to a friend, show the finished copy to a friend (relative, employee) before your direct mail piece is sent. What is *his* (or *her*) reaction?

3. *Do write several headlines.* Your odds of success increase the more headlines you write. And then pick and choose the one that tells and sells best. (For more on this, see Chapter 13, "Off With Their Head!")

4. *Do list benefits.* Tell all the advantages. And disadvantages. (What happens to the customer if he does *not* buy?)

5. *Do be specific.* If you are selling a technical product, list the specifications. Great for those who want to know. Those who don't want to know will be impressed. Tell the reader *exactly* what they will receive.

6. *Do count the number of times you use the word "you."* Here's an example of the importance of using the word "YOU" (the caps are ours) from a letter from the Book-of-the-Month Club:

Once YOU start shopping in America's Bookstore—YOU'LL be enjoying the most dependable reading reminder system in the world. YOU'LL be kept regularly informed of important new books, and given ample opportunity to choose the ones YOU want. YOU'LL soon come to depend on the Book-of-the-Month Club's thrifty shop-at-home service. Without leaving YOUR home, YOU can window-shop, browse and buy—and have the books YOU want delivered straight to YOUR door. And by continuing YOUR membership past the trial period, YOU'LL be eligible for our unique Book-Dividend plan.

John Caples, VP of Batten, Barton, Durstine & Osborn, once examined the most successful ads ever written. He found the word "you" far and above all the rest. If you added up the two words "you" and "your," it appears in nearly *half* of the winning ads.*

7. *Do write in the present tense.* As much as possible. Things that are in the past are . . . in the past. Forgotten. A long time ago. Not pertinent to *today.* Be active, not passive.

8. *Do write in simple phrases.* Keep paragraphs short and sentences shorter.

9. *Do include testimonials where possible.* Every advertisement has the same problem: "Is it true?" If you say a fact about your product it means one thing. If a customer says the same fact, it is far more believable.

10. *Do urge immediate action.* Give a time when the offer ends. Tell them to come and try and see and, of course, buy. Hurry. Quick. Fast.

Make Sure You Don't . . .

1. *Don't wait for inspiration.* Start writing by writing. When George Bernard Shaw was asked by a young man how to become a famous writer, Shaw answered, "Write." Sinclair Lewis said, "The art of writing is the art of applying the seat of the pants to the seat of the chair." So sit down and . . . write!

2. *Don't exaggerate.* Vrest Orton tells of the time he started in the mail order business. He visited L. L. Bean at his home in Freeport, Maine, and asked for advice. Said Bean, "Make sure the story isn't better than the store."

His point: Don't stretch the facts. Just tell the advantages to the customer of buying your product. If the product seems even *better* than what you wrote, your next ad will be an even bigger success.

3. *Don't use timeworn words.* Avoid the circus adjectives of "outstanding," "terrific," "fantastic." People tend to yawn at those words.

4. *Don't use time worn phrases.* "Once in a lifetime," "red as a rose," and "clear as water" are old and will make your merchandise appear old. Exception: If you can re-phrase them in a fun way. We recently did a promotion of clothing imported from Finland with the successful headline: "And now . . . the big Finnish!"

*For an awards-winning, results-proven letter using the word "You" twenty-seven times on just the first page, see Ed McClean's *Newsweek* letter in Chapter 7.

5. *Don't patronize.* Never imply you are doing the reader a favor by telling them about your product. And don't talk down. Do not imply you know more about your product than the reader does. Does that make it too difficult for them to learn?

6. *Don't print your letter.* Type it and have the typewritten copy photocopied. That's OK. But when you print a letter, you are writing to everyone instead of to someone.

7. *Don't try to be funny.* Humor is fine in a headline, in a TV sketch. But direct mail is different. It is very personal. That which makes you laugh may make your customer ask, "I wonder what they meant by that" or worse, consider your humor in bad taste.

8. *Don't think of your direct mailer as just a direct mailer. Think of it as a salesman.* Because . . . that's what it really is.

9. *Don't assume everyone knows what you know.* List all the facts even if you *think* your reader knows them. They will not mind being reminded.

10. *Don't give up.* Even if your last mailing piece did not do as well as you thought and/or hoped it would, the next one may do twice as well. The more you do, the more you will learn and the more comfortable you will feel about writing.

6
Off With Their Head!

Seven out of ten people will read the headline on your direct mailer.

But only three out of ten will keep on reading.

The headline is a most important part of your direct mail piece because it is at this point the reader decides whether or not they will continue reading from the top of your mailer to the copy that follows.

Your headline should have one of two appeals (best of all, both).

1. The headline should *promise a benefit*.
2. The headline should *provoke curiosity*.

David Ogilvy, founder of Ogilvy and Mather, one of the world's greatest advertising agencies, tells of the time he gathered his new copywriters into a room and said, "Ladies and gentemen, when you have written the headline for your ad, you have spent 75 percent of your client's money."

What was he saying? This: unless you capture the readers' attention up front and hold their interest, you will not create a desire to buy.

Readership surveys show that the average person will spend about four seconds on a newspaper page. One, two, three, four, turn the page. And in those four seconds the readers will glance at the headlines on the news columns *before* they look at the headlines on the ads—yours included. Unless your headline promises a benefit and provokes curiosity they will miss your message.

You can have the most fascinating, interesting, makes-me-want-to-buy copy in your ad. But if the headline does not stop me and keep me reading, that great copy will never be read.

Remember: In an average newspaper, your headline competes for attention with about 300 *other* headlines.

Bill Jayme, one of America's best direct mail advertising writers, once told us he spends about one-third of his time just thinking about the headline. The rest of the time goes into the multi-page hundreds of words that follows. His theory: What good does it do to write the best copy in the world if no one bothers to read past the headline?*

John Caples, Vice President of BBDO and a member of the Advertising Hall of Fame, once put together a series of different headlines for the same product—a retirement insurance plan from Phoenix Mutual. He found to his amazement that by simply changing the headline, he could double, triple, and in one test, receive *twenty times* the response of the original headline . . . just by using a new (and obviously more effective) headline.

Think of your headline as a good salesman in your business. Headlines command attention by offering the customer a reason to buy. The best ads and direct mailers are the ones that sell—not necessarily the ones that win awards.

John Kennedy, one of the greatest advertising copywriters in advertising history, applied for his first job by sending a note to Albert Lasker, president of the Lord & Thomas advertising agency, saying, "I have the best definition for advertising you have ever seen."

Intrigued, the agency head invited him to his office and asked what it was. Kennedy answered, "Advertising is salesmanship in print."

He got the job.

What that means: A good ad is one that sells. And selling begins with first impressions.

The headline on the envelope of your mailer competes with the other direct mail envelopes in the mailbox. This means you must know the techniques, words, concepts that work most of the time in the writing of the headline on the outside of your envelope or the beginning of your letter.

Here are ten ways to develop good headline have-its.

1. Have it appeal to self-interest.
2. Have it arouse curiosity.
3. Have it for the right audience.
4. Have it easy to understand.
5. Have it newsworthy.
6. Have it believable.
7. Have it produce quick results.
8. Have it specific.
9. Have it something of value.
10. Have it well-known.

Let's take them one at a time and see how they work.

1. Have it appeal to self-interest. What benefit does the headline offer

*Asked to come up with an attention-grabbing headline for the outside of an envelope carrying subscription letters for a new restaurant magazine, he wrote: "How much should you tip when you're planning to pocket the ashtray?"

me? The best-selling headline of all times—*How to Win Friends and Influence People,* the title of Dale Carnegie's book—was the third title tried. And it has resulted in one of the best sellers of all times. Because *everyone* wants to have friends. And influence people.

"How to make a million dollars in mail order."

"How to lose 10 pounds in 10 days."

"How to retire on $25,000 a year."

"Are you spending $10 a week too much for food?"

At the end of this chapter we have listed some best-selling headlines through the years. Look at them. Study them. Adopt and adapt them for your direct mail for your business.

2. Have it arouse curiosity. Stop your reader with a statement that makes him ask, "How can *that* be?" And/or, "What do they mean by that?" And/or, "Does that mean what I think it means?"

Examples . . .

"Do you wonder how we can sell an all-wool shetland sweater for less than $15?"

"How to look younger in 14 days."

"How many of these 20 questions can you answer correctly?"

This last one follows a basic direct mail guideline: get the customer involved.

As soon as you have the customer not only reading but also have them acting ("Peel off this label" . . . "Fill in this coupon" . . . "Cut along this line") then your results will increase dramatically.

Important: You must answer the question you raise in the headline in the copy that follows. And the answer must make logical sense. *Because* you are having a sale. *Because* you made a special purchase. *Because* you are offering your customers a pre-season chance to buy before you advertise to the world. The customers curiosity must be satisfied by your explanation otherwise they simply will not respond now and, more importantly, they will have real skepticism on any future mailings from you. A shocking statistic that recently appeared in print revealed that 90 percent of Americans do *not* associate the word "trust" with the word "business."

And "trust" a key word in direct mail. Always remember direct mail's *greatest* strength is the personal relationship between you and your customer. If you arouse your customer's curiosity in the headline, answer it logically and sensibly in the copy that follows to create that trust.

3. Have it for the right audience. Never forget the two most important ingredients in a successful direct mail package are (a) the List and (b) the product or service.

The List. You start off with a giant advantage, the list. Your own customers. People who trust and believe in you because they have invested their money with you in the past. They know you.

The professionals call these names a "data base." Don't be confused by this term. It only means the list of your customer's names.

Your customers are obviously your right audience. When looking to expand your mailing list and using new lists, make sure these new names are as close as possible to your present customers in terms of age/salary/ location/lifestyle.

Again, you will find the professionals using words like geographics, demographics, psychographics. They are simply another way of saying to make sure your names are similar to your present customers in terms of age/salary/where they live . . . etc.

The product or service. This means you do not suggest or recommend a product the customer does *not* want. Too much waste of time and (your) money. Start with what customers are presently buying from you. You start with this built-in advantage.

If a customer is near retirement you do not offer the same package you would to a newlywed. Or grass seed to apartment dwellers. Some of the direct mail experts say the best mailer is only 20 percent devoted to creativity. The other 80 percent is divided equally between the right product or service . . . and the right list.

4. Have it easy to understand. Most of us talk in two languages, one when we are talking to one another, the second when we sit down to write something. We suddenly become a different person, very erudite and much more difficult to understand. When writing a headline (or copy) make it easy to understand. Do *not* use words peculiar to your specific kind of business. Each industry has a jargon that only insiders know. What will work in a trade magazine will not work in a general publication or a wide spread direct mail campaign.

And do *not* talk in terms of the *features* of the product. But talk in terms of *benefits*. Forget the detailed analysis. Say what the item will do for the reader.

What does that mean?

If a jacket is down-filled say, "Twice the warmth at half the weight."

If an insurance policy has lower rates for non-smokers say, "Double the coverage for the same premium."

If the tires are steel belted, say, "When you're away from home, your family is riding on the safest tires ever designed."

A recent bank headline said, "Every officer in our establishment receives a thrill whenever a loan is consummated."

Who talks like that?

Now, if the headline said, "Here's the money you need to open your shop" . . . well, everyone understands *that*.

5. Have it newsworthy. Look at the direct mail pieces you receive in the mail. Notice how many times you see these words in headlines: *New*.

Announcing. For the first time. Introducing. Free.

There's a reason. They work.

Cereals and soups are constantly promoted as "New and improved." So are toothpaste, soap and gasoline.

If you can tie in a recent news story with your product, that works well. If the paper runs a story about your business, clip it out and reprint it as a mailer for prospective customers with the headline, "Did you see this story in the paper?"

Customers respond favorably to that which is new, the latest, just out. Everyone wants to be at the front of the line when the store opens.

Some writers say a headline is like a billboard. Once you have more than six or eight words, it is not read. Not true.

New York University's School of Retailing ran headline tests working with a large department store. Their conclusion: headlines with ten words *or more* sold more than short headlines.

The trick: The words must contain *news or information.*

6. *Have it believable.* The headline that begins, "This is your last chance to . . ." is the one I never finish reading. I know a similar (or better) offer will follow in the next mail.

The mailer with the headline that says, "How to make a million dollars in your spare time" quickly finds its way to the nearest wastepaper basket.

A recent advertisement for light bulbs did not work. The photograph showed the top of a light bulb broken off with the headline, "Don't bite off more than you can chew." I was tempted to write them and tell them I bit off only as much as shown in the picture and now I had this pain in my stomach and my attorney said . . .

An ad for truck sales showed a truck in the middle of a sesame seed bun with the headline, "More than one million sold." A take off on the McDonald's theme but I really do not want to buy a truck that fits inside a sesame seed bun.

We agree with David Ogilvy's line, "The customer is not a moron. She's your wife."

Writers who look for the cute (and irrelevant) phrase, the clever pun, the gimmick angle wind up with headlines that are often looked at . . . but not believed.

If you offer a well-known product at too low a price, the customer asks herself, "What's the gimmick? It simply doesn't make sense." It is not believable. And therefore it's ignored. Tossed away.

7. *Have it produce quick results.* Americans are accustomed to speed. The success of the newspaper *USA Today* is because the format closely parallels the nightly TV news. A condensation of what happened that day without too much detail. Everything complete on one page. And preferably in one or two paragraphs.

If you can show how someone can lose weight quickly, make money quickly, be successful in a short period of time in a believable manner, people will read what you have to say.

8. Have it specific. What does "Half-price sale" mean? Yes, it means one half the original price. But if you do not say the original price . . . , what does "half-price sale" mean? Half of what?

When banks offer savings in terms of percentages . . . what do the percentages mean? If they would offer the return in dollars . . . well, that we understand.

A Texas bank did just that. Did people really "understand" the numbers game the banks were playing in their ads? That was the question asked by Doug McDougal, marketing officer of Victoria National Bank in Victoria, Texas. His competitive market included four banks, three savnigs and loans within a 60,000 population.

The problem: His bank was the *last* to advertise money market certificates. When they finally decided to do it, they were faced with the problem of what to do differently from the competition?

They examined all the ads and they noticed that all the competition advertised percentages. No one advertised *dollars*.

This was their 11-word headline: "Deposit $10,000 today. Walk out with $10,476 in only six months."

McDougal's advertising budget was $1,450. This gave the bank two newspaper ads every week for seven weeks. Here's what happened, in Doug's words: "We had been taking in $70,000 daily in new money market certificates before the ad broke. That figure jumped immediately to *$250,000* daily. One day we sold $521,000. Many customers came in with the ad in their hand."

In one year the bank took in more than four *million* dollars in new money for money market certificates.

Not bad for an investment of $1,450. And simply because they talked in specific terms of dollars rather than percentages.

Barney's clothing store in New York City has been running twice-a year sales with the headline, "100 Reasons to Shop Barney's Summer Sale" or "100 Reasons to Shop Barney's Winter Sale."

They list 100 items they have on sale. The customers keep on reading and reading and reading . . . and then buying and buying and buying.

People have a strange attraction to numbers. From the Ten Commandments to the "Seven out of ten people who . . ." to "The 19 reasons why" to the "16 people who believe that . . . ," not only do people read the headline and then start reading the copy . . . but more amazingly, they have to read down to the last number mentioned.

The more specific you are in your headline, the more selective you are in targeting your audience.

"An important message to men who are losing their hair . . ." "How college students can earn their tuition this summer."

The more specific you are, the more you attract the right audience to buy your product.

9. *Have it something of value.* The cosmetics people have this down to an exact science. They call it "purchase with purchase." If you buy one of their products, you receive a gift for free or for a fraction of its true value.

Offer benefits you have that make you separate and different from and put you in front of the competition: free parking, free gift wrapping, free delivery, free monogramming . . .

- Make it a collectible. ("If you bought this anniversary plate five years ago for $10, you could sell it for $50 today.")
- Make it priceworthy. ("Would you buy this $75 designer blouse for $29?")
- Make it within a time limit ("After June 1st, this computer will sell for $500. Now it is yours for $350")
- Make it fulfill a dream ("To men who want to quit work some day.")
- Make it fulfill a weakness ("How I improved my memory in one evening.")
- Make it eliminate a drudgery ("How to prepare a complete and delicious meal in only 60 minutes.")

10. Have it well known. David Ogilvy said, "Include the brand name in the headline." A good idea. Whenever possible. But putting in the name just for putting in the name is not good enough.

If your name has a reason for being there, fine. Because you are the first to . . . because you are the place where . . . because you are known for . . . all good reasons. But simply putting your store's name in *without a reason* may make you feel good but will not do a thing for your customer.

Brand names are important because they make the reader feel comfortable. Readers know about a specific brand and will respond in a more positive manner than to an unfamiliar brand. (See Chapter 3, *The Five Reasons People Buy.*)

Using testimonials fills the same well known need. Customers react positively to endorsements by well-known people. Otherwise why are all these advertising agencies paying all that money? Many sport celebrities earn much more on the testimonial circuit than on the playing field. The reason why: They are well known.

TOOLBOX

A Baker's Dozen of Headline Words

Now that you know the reasons why headlines work, are there certain words that seem to work in headlines better than other words?

Yes.

The following words are seen in the most successful headlines. They trigger positive emotional responses from your customer. A survey of words most commonly used in successful headlines came up with this baker's dozen. Try one (or more) next time you are writing the headline for your next direct mailer.

Here they are.

1. *Free.* Still number one. Everyone wants to know what they can have at no cost.

2. *New.* Everyone wants to have the latest, what is "in," be the first on the block with the latest car, dress, hairdo, latest technology. Great word (well, unless you're selling antiques).

3. *Now.* Gives a sense of immediacy. Quick. Hurry. Don't be late.

4. *Wanted.* What's wanted? By whom? For how much? Where?

5. *Announcing.* Something just happened and you're the first to know.

6. *How.* Most often seen as *"How to . . ."* and followed by a strong benefit.

7. *Win.* Which accounts for the tremendous success of sweepstakes, bingo parlors, Las Vegas and Atlantic City.

8. *Guarantee.* We all want to be reassured. There is no risk if I buy from you. Tell me how long you have been in busines. Make the guarantee big, bold, prominent (near the order blank if you are asking for an order) and *simple.*

9. *Easy.* If what you have to sell takes less effort to do a job I am presently doing, say so. (Or by making it easy for the reader to buy your product.)

10. *You.* People are interested in themselves. The more you use *you* in your headlines the more you will increase your readership. (That's five times in just one sentence.)

11. *Save.* Everyone wants to save something, somewhere, sometime.

12. *At last.* From the song of the same name. Has the feel of something that has happened that you always wanted to happen.

13. *Breakthrough.* Joe Sugarman, one of the country's top copywriters, says every time he uses the word "breakthrough" in his headlines, his sales increase. He has used "Printer Breakthrough" for the past ten years in his catalogs for the same calculator, and it works every time. Other businesses have copied Sugarman's magic word with excellent results.

(Here are some examples of product from his recent catalogs. The word works well . . . with almost *any* product. Try "breakthrough" on a product or service you sell in your next direct mailer. But make sure you tell of some new, different or unusual feature that makes it a . . . "breakthrough."

Now that you have read this far, congratulations! You are now an expert in headlines!

(To see how good you really are, try the test on the next page to see if you can tell . . . "Which Headline Pulled Best?")

The Questions

John Caples, a member of the advertising Hall of Fame once did this test: he wrote two headlines for the same product. The two ads were identical in art and copy. Only the headlines were different. One headline drew 19 times the response of the other!

Through the years, by testing, he would advertise a product with two different headlines. The difference in results was amazing. And often the exact opposite of what Caples had predicted.

We were fascinated with the idea. Since we write nearly 300 headlines a year. We tried the testing. And it worked for us, too. Here are some of the headlines Caples wrote. And some we wrote. Which pulled best? Can you tell?

1. □ A. How a man of 40 can retire in 15 years
   □ B. Get a vacation with pay
2. □ A. What's new in summer sandwiches?
   □ B. Guest for supper? What shall I offer them?
   □ C. Heard about those new canopies?
3. □ A. Next 90 days can change your life
   □ B. How I got a better job
4. □ A. Keep your dog **safe** this summer
   □ B. Don't poison your dog
5. □ A. Buy three books for 99¢–get one free!
   □ B. Buy any of these four books for only 99¢
6. □ A. 60 days ago they called me "baldy"
   □ B. If I can't grow hair for you in 30 days, you get your money back
7. □ A. Get rid of money worries for good
   □ B. Here's one question you shouldn't ask your wife.
8. □ A. Here's a strange way to learn music
   □ B. A few months ago I couldn't play a note
9. □ A. How you can retire on a guaranteed home income for life
   □ B. A vacation that lasts the rest of your life
10. □ A. How $7 started me on the road to $20,000 a year
    □ B. Some $20,000 jobs are looking for applicants

11. □ A. This fascinating literary circle now open to you
    □ B. Can you talk about books with the rest of them?
12. □ A. Why good dancers are more popular than walk-arounds
    □ B. How a faux pas made me popular
13. □ A. We disappointed so many people last year because we couldn't deliver these individually made hats for Christmas. So we decided to tell you about them early.
    □ B. Only thirty days left to buy this hat for Christmas
14. □ A. The old fashioned metal hook & eye slicker at an old fashioned price: $8.50
    □ B. Can't lose this raincoat 'cause it has their name on it.
15. □ A. This is the paper for you
    □ B. How to get the Los Angeles Times delivered to your house
16. □ A. How to make your food taste better
    □ B. How to get your cooking bragged about
17. □ A. The gift that comes 12 times a year
    □ B. How to do your Christmas shopping in five minutes
18. □ A. Announcing an important revision of the Bible
    □ B. Most important Bible news in 340 years
19. □ A. To every woman who would like a career in interior design
    □ B. Can you spot these 7 common decorating sins?
20. □ A. Tension headache?
    □ B. When doctors have headaches, what do they do?

The Answers

How to score:

1-10: remember when you were bad in school you had to write "I will be good" 100 times on the blackboard. If this is your score, you have to write 100 headlines for every ad you do for the next month.

10-15: You're one of the crowd. Are happy to do your job and go home to the wife, children, dog and fireplace.

16-20: Are you available to work for us? You're real good...

1. A The winner is a rifle bullet headline. "B"is a shotgun headline. This ad was tested three ways: (1) readership (2) coupon returns (3) sales made by salesman calling on coupons. Ad "B" got higher **readership** but "A" got higher coupons and made more sales. Did not do well in total readership because it limited its audience not only to men but to men aged 40. Ad B had a greater audience.

2. A This is an ad for Spam. Winning headline has "new". Is timely ('summer').
   • Guests for supper – (Would you serve them Spam?)
   • What are canopies? (Is it a can of peas?)

3. A People thought "B" was a help-wanted ad.

4. A Brought 56% better response. How many dog owners want to **poison** their dogs?

5. A Ran after control (B) stopped pulling as well for Doubleday book clubs.

6. A Selects right audience. Ad "B" does not select audience and the headline guarantee is a suggestion the product will not work.

7. A Promises a benefit "B" does not.

8. A Arouses curiosity ("strange way") and promises a benefit ("learn music").

9. A "B" is misleading.

10. A "B" sounds like an ad from an employment agency

11. B Selects right audience and promises a benefit. "B" sounds like you're joining a literary club

12. B "More popular" implies a benefit. "Faux pas" arouses curiosity

13. B Pulled ten times as well. First ad sold 9 hats the day the ad ran. Second ad sold **90** hats the day the ad ran. The word "disappointed" was negative so they stopped reading. Second headline told the story more simply.

14. B Pulled ten times as well! It struck a very responsible chord to parents whose children's identical yellow slicker raincoats were misplaced or picked up by another child in error. These raincoats were monogrammed with the child's name. (SIDE NOTE: These raincoats cost twice as much ($17.00). Price was overcome by desire.)

15. B Pulled three times as well (first ran 20 years ago – **still being** run and copied by NY Times and Wall St. Journal).

16. B Implies you can improve food you serve and offers demand of praise (Pulled 42% better.)

17. B Quick, easy for you. "B" promises benefit to receiver of gift **not** to you. Doubled sale results of "B".

18. B "B" pulled 71% better. Both ran in NY Daily News. **340** years carries conviction & implies news of great consequence.

19. B Arouses curiosity. Involves reader. Headline "A" is limited audience.

20. B Outpulled "A". Both attracts audience with "headaches". But what do doctors do? Attracts curiosity.

7
I'm Gonna Sit Right Down and Write Myself a Letter

October 1

Dear Mrs. Brown,
   I sell good meat and poultry.

Yours sincerely,
Albert Hawkins
Butcher

October 8

Dear Mrs. Brown,
   My customers can be sure of prompt delivery of good meat and poultry.

Yours sincerely,
Albert Hawkins
Butcher

October 15

Dear Mrs. Brown,
   It doesn't cost much.

Yours sincerely,
Albert Hawkins
Butcher

October 22

Dear Mrs. Brown,

I said it doesn't cost much to buy my good meat and poultry and
have it immediately delivered.

Yours sincerely,
Albert Hawkins
Butcher

THE SERIES OF LETTERS above was actually mailed to a group of home
owners in a rural village in England. And, we are glad to report, Mr.
Hawkins the butcher did a land office business.

Why?

Because . . . he wrote a personal letter to residents in his selling area,
told them who he was, what he did and the advantages of buying from him.
And reminded them again. And reminded them again. And reminded them
again. And . . .

Writing a letter is the simplest form of direct mail. It is the definition
of direct mail. The letter is *mailed directly* to your customer.

In an earlier chapter we spoke of the person-to-person, me-and-thee
relationship *only* possible in direct mail.

Direct mail shows your customer you care. You have taken the time to
tell her something that they know about first.

Direct mail is the medium that shows up your strong points: Friendli-
ness, reliability, service and, most important, the amount of personal attention lavished on the customer.

Now, let's see how it works. And how you can do it starting . . . today.

It is not complicated. The easiest directions are the title of this chapter.
Sit down and write a letter to your customers as if you were writing a
letter to yourself. Make it chatty, informal, comfortable, newsworthy.

That means you do *not* begin with the time-honored and boring sentences.

"In response to your letter of the 13th inst. . . . ."

"Pursuant to your notification of employment opportunities . . ."

"I am in receipt of your letter of . . ."

Begin with something to capture the reader's attention and interest.
A story. A saying. An offer. A something that will make him stop . . . and
read.

It can be a headline like a story in the newspaper. It can be a question
to make the reader wonder, "What's this all about?" It can promise a
benefit if he keeps on reading.

Ask yourself if your letter passes the *stop, look* and *listen* test.

STOP!

We once worked for a builder of houses. We went with him when he visited a piece of ground where he planned to build. We watched him walk over the ground. We heard him check for the depth of the water. We saw him work and re-work building plans.

A closet was sketched in, then erased. A bathroom was moved and re-moved on the blueprint. The final positioning of the house on the lot was changed and re-changed. There were the calls to the electrical com pany. There was the clearing of the title of the land.

One week later we said, "When do we start building?"

"Start building?" he answered, "that's the easy part."

Mailing the letter is the easy part. Knowing everything to do before the letter is mailed, the preparation, this is the tedious work. But . . . it's the work that makes your letter successful.

You can't write a letter until you first know what you want to accomplish.

First, decide what you want to do:

Sell merchandise? Introduce a new product? A new salesman? A new address? Tell someone who you are? Have someone vote for you? Ask questions for a survey?

Write down, in one sentence, what you want your finished letter to do.

Then, list the selling points and benefits. What are you doing? The same job the architect did a few paragraphs ago—sketching plans for the finished product. This goes here. And that goes there.

Your letter, like a story, a play, a speech, has three parts:

A beginning.
A middle
An end.

It's really repeating the three-step formula:

• Say what you are going to say.
• Say it.
• Say what you said.

Your letter should follow these three steps in a logical sequence. *Your beginning* makes a dramatic statement ("What will happen to me if I read this?") *Your middle* explains in more detail what you just said ("Oh, so that's what they mean"). And reinforces your basic selling point ("Hmmm, look what happened to others who bought this"). *Your* end persuades and finally convinces ("Quick, where's my pen to fill in this order blank").

Having your letter follow a regular, organized presentation makes it easier for the customer to follow along. The clothing salesman does not show shirts then stop half-way through to bring socks. Then stop to show ties. Doesn't work. He sells the suit, then the shirt, then the tie, then the socks. One flows from the other.

This rhythm in face-to-face selling works in word-to-word selling. You make a statement . . . then proceed to prove that statement.

But you cannot start until you first stop. Ask yourself:

WHAT DO I WANT THE READER TO DO AFTER HE READS THIS LETTER?

LOOK!

What does your letter "look" like?

If you write one long paragraph to fill each page, the letter is not too attractive to look at, much less read.

Keep your sentences short. Keep words to one or two syllables. Keep paragraphs to two or three sentences.

Avoid adjectives. Use action verbs. Eliminate unnecessary words that slow down the reader like "that" . . . "a" . . . "an."

Write or typewrite your letter. Don't print it. (Who *prints* a letter? Answer: Those who don't want it read.) Consider hand-written notes in the margin. They serve the same purpose as those little sub-headlines you see in printed copy. Gives the eye a rest from reading. Summarizes what you're about to read.

Use color. Sign your name in blue ink instead of black. What difference does that make? This: Your name will now stand out because the rest of the letter is in black type. And blue is an accepted color for signatures. Simple? Sure. And it works.

Use those figures on top of the number keys on your typewriter. Push down the shift lock key and you'll discover ways to express amazement!!!! And dashes to hook-things-together. Slashes for either/or choices. And another way to say &. You can whisper quietly in your letter (by saying something inside here) or yell louder by SAYING IT LIKE THIS.

The little dot can be a period ending a sentence like this. Or to keep you reading between sentences . . . Like this . . . And this. Or to begin a series of reasons-why like:

- This reason here and
- Then this reason here.

Underlining your words points out an interesting fact <u>if this was an interesting fact.</u>

LISTEN

After you have finished writing your letter, read it aloud. "Listen" to it as though you were someone who received it rather than wrote it.

All the direct mail rule books say, "Write as though you were talking." or "Write a letter to your Aunt Minny."

That's all well and good and to be desired. But the truth is you want to capture the "feeling" of writing that way. Not actually write the way you talk. If so, each letter would run about 40 pages. The average person talks at the rate of 150 words a minute. One full page like this will take two minutes to read aloud. Five pages is ten minutes or more. That's a long time. You better have one good reason after another for them to keep on reading the pages.

Listen to the "sound" of your letter. Is your reader "comfortable" with what he is reading? We mentioned it in the last chapter, and we repeat: Most of us have two languages. One for talking. Another for writing. We suddenly become academic English majors when we put pen to paper or fingers to typewriter. This may turn the reader off. If he is not comfortable reading, he will not like the letter or the product you want him to buy.

It also works in reverse: does your letter sound as though *you* like your reader? If so, it will come out in how you write. Be warm. Be friendly. Show the enthusiasm you have for your merchandise. Share the belief you have in the benefits they will receive. All this comes about in the words you use and how you use them.

Remember: Direct mail is a very special relationship between you and your customer. It is a me-and-thee approach. It is the two of you sharing some information. Can't happen unless you share common interests.

And even though you can achieve some nuances of speech by using the character keys on the typewriter, it is impossible for the printed word to gesture, roll its eyes, burst into laughter, cry or shrug its shoulders.

Listen to the arguments you make for buying in your letter. Would they convince you? Have you anticipated your readers' questions/objections and come up with answers? Have you given them enough information to buy? Have you given them a guarantee that they must be satisfied or they receive their money back?

Have you given them a reason to act now? Quick! Today. And then have you given them several ways to buy? Cash. Charge. Time payment.

Never ask if they want to buy; offer different ways they *can* buy. And if you think of one more item you forgot to include, save it. There's a special place. One that has the highest "listening" potential in your letter. And that is *after* your signature. It is called the P.S.

After the headline, the P.S. is the best read part of a letter ("Aha! I wonder what they forgot to say in the letter?"). Make the P.S. a summary of what you said. Or include one more benefit. Or repeat the most important benefit. Or remind them of the deadline they must act by.

At this point, if you think all this is overwhelming, relax. The key words are: Are you natural?

Are you yourself?

Are you writing as if you were writing to *one* person and not to your hundreds or thousands or tens of thousands of customers?

Stop. Sit down. Decide what you're going to say. How you're going to say it. What you want to leave in and leave out.

Look. Does the letter "look" interesting to read?

Listen. How does it "sound" to you? Does it give a clarion call to buy?

The Seven Steps to Writing a Successful Business Letter

Why do some letters work and others not?

One accepted technique is explained by Direct Marketing expert Bob Stone in his excellent book *Successful Direct Marketing Methods*. He says, "This is a letter-writing formula that has served me well."

That was good enough for us.

And so we examined and analyzed award-winning and results-proven letters. (We've included some in the TOOLBOX section of this chapter.)

In taking them apart we find they all seem to follow his seven-step formula. (Well, almost all. Nothing works *always.**)

1. Promise a benefit. Up front. Right in the beginning. Award-winning copywriter Bill Jayme asks,

"Does the lead on your letter say 'Read me because' or 'Read me despite . . .'?"

What positive event will happen to the reader who keeps on reading?

2. Enlarge on the benefit. The opening benefit is short, concise, summarized. It could be a headline on the top of the letter. It could be a strong, attention-demanding first paragraph.

Now, the next few paragraphs explain in greater detail what is included in this benefit.

---

*At the turn of the century in Russia, the rabbi was judge and jury in the small villages. One day a new young rabbi came in to learn the job. "You came the right day," said the older rabbi. "A husband and wife have come to me with a problem. Listen and you will see how I solve it." First the husband told his story, The rabbi listened carefully and when the husband finished, the rabbi said, "You're right. You're absolutely right." Then the wife told her side of the story. Again the rabbi listened and when she finished, the rabbi said, "You're right. You're absolutely right." The young rabbi interrupted. "Wait a minute," he said. "You listened to the husband and said he was right. You listened to the wife and said she was right. They both can't be right." The older rabbi thought, looked at him and said, "You know what—you're right. You're absolutely right."

3. Be specific. The best way to explain this is to have you look at a Sears catalog. Descriptions of merchandise are short and concise but they tell you what you want to know. Colors. Sizes. Washable? Price. Does it work in 20-below weather?

4. Give proof. Testimonials are good. And not necessarily only from famous people. Everyone knows the people who endorse products receive some sort of payment for the words they say. (Even though the Federal government says if a celebrity gives a testimonial, he better be ready to prove he uses the product.) But a name of a real person in a real community also works.

5. What happens if they don't act. Remember fear of loss has a far greater appeal than promise of gain. That's why there is so much insurance sold. And that is the reason cut-off dates are important in your letter. Spurs the customer to immediate action. Phrases like, "The free camera is yours only if you act before . . ." are powerful involvement tools if they are true.

6. Repeat. The close of the sale. Where the salesperson summarizes and repeats all the benefits of buying he listed during the entire sales talk. Short, concise and gives reasons for buying . . . *now!*

7. AFTO. The salesman's critical concluding phrase: *A*sk *F*or *T*he *O*rder.

Tell the customer what to do. "Cut along this line." "Print your name here." "Fold and seal." "Please check appropriate payment box: Visa, Mastercard, American Express, Diner's Club, Check . . ."

Summary:

The seven steps to writing a successful letter are:

1. Promise a benefit.
2. Enlarge on the benefit.
3. Be specific.
4. Give proof.
5. What happens if they don't act?
6. Repeat.
7. AFTO.

What makes a good letter writer?

Someone who is articulate. Who puts himself in the position of the reader. Who can discover the individual, yours-alone, selling proposition in your product. Who has respect for the reader's good sense. Who knows how to keep the reader first attracted, then interested, then committed to keep on reading . . . and then buying.

All of these ingredients—and more—are found in the talented team of Bill Jayme and his designer-partner, Heikki Ratalahti.

We include some of Jayme's award-winning and (more important) results-proven letters in this TOOLBOX section with letters from other top writers like Joe Sugarman and Ed McLean.

The reason for these letters: To show you how the best writers write. Everyone learns by imitation. The learning pianist buys the recordings of the great masters and listens to the nuances and shadings of a particular phrase until the groove becomes worn with the repetition.

Next time you visit an art gallery, you will see, tucked away in one of the corners, a young artist, palette in hand, canvas stretched tight, carefully recapturing the mood and color of the famous painting before him.

The great writers, artists, musicians, merchants, business people become great not only by using their talent but, in the beginning, by copying that which preceded. And, having copied and learned, they re-make what has been done into their own individual tapestry.

It is not enough simply to do that which has been done before. When you do that you are merely someone else. It is important to learn from the experts and then add the necessary ingredients unique to you.

Copying the successful direct mail letters that follow is not enough for you. For then you are merely copying the painting on the wall of the art gallery. It tells someone else's story, not yours.

The letter that winds up in the mailbox of your customer must be familiar-looking, yet yours alone. It should not and cannot be another. If it's only a copy, you lose your identity and become someone else instead.

And so when reading what follows, see what others have done and why. Then pick and choose and adopt and adapt to *your* business. When you have done that, you are on the road to success.

When an oil fire rages out of control, a hurry-up phone call is placed to Red Adair, who has proven he knows how to solve this type of problem.

When a theatrical production is in trouble, a voice cries out, "Call 'Doc' Simon." And author and play doctor Neil Simon is called upon to make the production work.

And when someone decides to launch a new magazine on the market place, the phrase soon heard is, "Call Bill Jayme."

The reason: The San Francisco-based Jayme-Ratalahti team has con--sistently launched successful publications with a combination of good illustrations and a great letter.

Together they create about fifteen pieces each year. They turn down about *three* times that number.

"In any good package," says Jayme, "nearly half the contents are not about the magazine but about the prospect's needs. I place myself in their shoes. What does a newly arrived Polish immigrant care to read about? Well, he wants to know if he should change his name, where he can learn English, how to find work," says Jayme. "I have to be an actor.

"I could transform myself into a 22-year-old pregnant woman if I had to . . ."

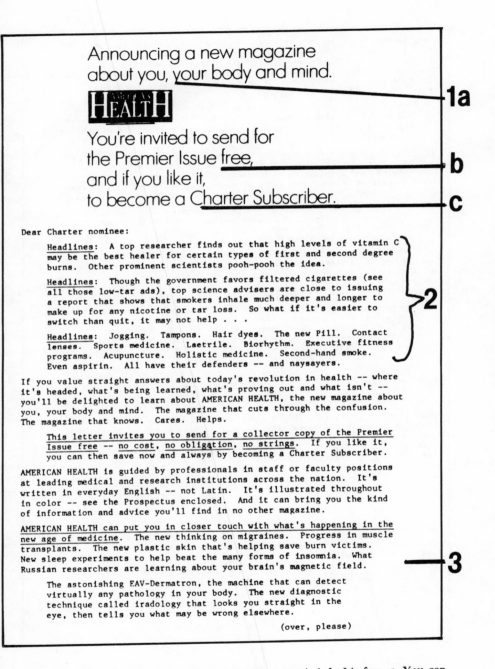

Announcing a new magazine
about you, your body and mind.

HEALTH

You're invited to send for
the Premier Issue free,
and if you like it,
to become a Charter Subscriber.

— 1a

— b

— c

Dear Charter nominee:

    Headlines: A top researcher finds out that high levels of vitamin C
may be the best healer for certain types of first and second degree
burns. Other prominent scientists pooh-pooh the idea.

    Headlines: Though the government favors filtered cigarettes (see
all those low-tar ads), top science advisers are close to issuing
a report that shows that smokers inhale much deeper and longer to
make up for any nicotine or tar loss. So what if it's easier to
switch than quit, it may not help . . .

    Headlines: Jogging. Tampons. Hair dyes. The new Pill. Contact
lenses. Sports medicine. Laetrile. Biorhythm. Executive fitness
programs. Acupuncture. Holistic medicine. Second-hand smoke.
Even aspirin. All have their defenders -- and naysayers.

2

If you value straight answers about today's revolution in health -- where
it's headed, what's being learned, what's proving out and what isn't --
you'll be delighted to learn about AMERICAN HEALTH, the new magazine about
you, your body and mind. The magazine that cuts through the confusion.
The magazine that knows. Cares. Helps.

    This letter invites you to send for a collector copy of the Premier
Issue free -- no cost, no obligation, no strings. If you like it,
you can then save now and always by becoming a Charter Subscriber.

AMERICAN HEALTH is guided by professionals in staff or faculty positions
at leading medical and research institutions across the nation. It's
written in everyday English -- not Latin. It's illustrated throughout
in color -- see the Prospectus enclosed. And it can bring you the kind
of information and advice you'll find in no other magazine.

AMERICAN HEALTH can put you in closer touch with what's happening in the
new age of medicine. The new thinking on migraines. Progress in muscle
transplants. The new plastic skin that's helping save burn victims.
New sleep experiments to help beat the many forms of insomnia. What
Russian researchers are learning about your brain's magnetic field.

— 3

    The astonishing EAV-Dermatron, the machine that can detect
virtually any pathology in your body. The new diagnostic
technique called iradology that looks you straight in the
eye, then tells you what may be wrong elsewhere.

                           (over, please)

1. Promise a Benefit: a. It's for you, your body, your mind. **b.** It's free. **c.** You can
become a Charter Subscriber. **2. Enlarge on the Benefit:** Each of these *headlines* tells
you in greater detail about stories that have a bearing on your body, your mind, your
health. **3. Be Specific:** Here are specific articles the magazine carries.

AMERICAN HEALTH can put you in closer touch with yourself. Why you have allergies. New eye exercises that improve vision. The therapeutic effects of talcum powder. Male menopause. Which sports are best for your body. Which foods impair -- not help -- nutrition. Which drugs have side effects like hair loss...or gain. What it means when you sneeze. Dream. Cry. Laugh. Get angry. Tired. Aroused.

How to know if your doctor keeps up. How to stop chronic snoring. How to turn 30 with grace. And 40. The seven-year itch -- fact or fancy. The benefits of fasting. ESP and diagnosis. New directions in healing and psychotherapy. Placebos. Don't laugh. They work.

AMERICAN HEALTH can save you money -- and worry. You're better equipped to handle minor emergencies without having to run to the doctor. You learn how to spot symptoms -- and whenever possible, how to treat them, or which specialist to see. You discover techniques for preventing illness through improved diet, more beneficial exercise, a more positive outlook. ⟶ **4**

You find out the truth about health insurance -- Blue Cross, Blue Shield, major medical. You learn how to negotiate doctor and hospital bills. How to save on prescription drugs. Which drugstore remedies work, and which don't.

AMERICAN HEALTH is being published every other month. Individual issues cost $2, or $12 a year. When you mail the enclosed card promptly, you get a mint copy of the Premier Issue free -- Volume I, Number One, the edition most prized by collectors, and the cornerstone of a home medical reference library you can build with your copies of AMERICAN HEALTH. ⟶ **6**

Save now and always. If you like this first issue, your price for a full year's subscription is only $9 for all five additional bi-monthly issues. Right away, you save $3 off the regular subscription price. And as a Charter Subscriber, you'll save more every time you renew -- always the lowest possible price, with a full refund guarantee at all times. ⟶ **7**

Risk free. But if you decide that AMERICAN HEALTH is not for you, just write "cancel" on the subscription bill, return it within two weeks, and that's that. You've spent nothing. You owe nothing. The Premier Issue is yours to keep free with our compliments.

SEND NO MONEY. "Health", Thomas Jefferson observed, "is worth more than learning." Our new magazine will see that you enjoy more of both. More information and background -- for more learning. More learning -- for more health and vitality. With so much to gain, and nothing to lose, shouldn't you at least have a look? Thank you!

All the best,

T. George Harris

T. George Harris
Editor-In-Chief

P.S. Early postmark. Only so many copies of the Premier Edition are being printed -- no more. In fairness to both subscribers and first issue collectors, requests will be filled on a first-come, first-served basis according to postmark. Avoid disappointment by returning the enclosed card as quickly as convenient. ⟶ **5**

GH/ac

AMERICAN HEALTH, 322 WEST 80TH STREET, NEW YORK, N Y 10024

---

4. Give Proof: Look at the money and worry you save when you subscribe. **5. What Happens if they Don't Act?** They lose the chance to be a charter subscriber. Authentic because of the phrase, "requests will be filled on a first-come, first-served basis." **6. Repeat:** The offer in the headline is repeated again. **7. Ask for the Order!**

See their letter that launched the publication *American Health*. This is an example of their work. Notice how it follows the Seven Steps.

More than 300,000 people bought a subscription to this magazine without ever seeing the magazine!

Now that you know the basics of writing a letter, let us graduate to the next step. The putting together of a direct mail *package*. **The letter is the most important.** But since you know how that works, lets' talk about a direct mail package which has five different parts.

Five "Givens" for a Successful Direct Mail Package

1. *The outside envelope.*
   - What have you given me to make me want to open and read more?
2. *The letter.*
   - What have you given me to make me want to keep on reading?
3. *The brochure.*
   - What have you given me so that I can read more about your offer?
4. *The order blank.*
   - What have you given me so I can buy now . . . at once?
5. *The return envelope.*
   - What have you given me to make it easy to send you back the order?

(On a business reply card, combine 4 and 5.)

An Example of How the Five "Givens" Work

Something is said to be "a given" when it is something expected. Having a clean environment, having a well-stocked store, having merchandise arrive when promised, they are all expected, accepted and each is a given in the operation of a successful business.

That does *not* mean they *always* happen.

It *does* mean they *should* happen.

And so it is with writing a successful direct mail package.

Most have at least five pieces to make them work to the best of their ability. (For a six-piece letter, see chapter 11) That's a "given."

Yes, some can have just two pieces (an envelope and a letter).

Yes, some can have ten pieces or more (with a stack of inserts tucked inside).*

* And in case you are wondering how many inserts are too many inserts, the answer is "when the postage goes up because there are too many." Other than that, tuck in as many as you can. Here's why: the more reasons you give someone to buy, the more you increase the odds of them buying.

But if you are looking for a direction that seems to work most of the time, make sure your package has the five basic pieces described on the previous page.

Let's look at them one by one:

1. The outside envelope. Almost all of your packages can be mailed third class. They should because of the savings in postage and because readership has little or no relationship to whether you mail first class or third class.

Use a window envelope. This way the person's name shows through (which means it does not have to be repeated on the envelope).

You can use questions on the envelope, each written to appeal in some manner. At least one will make the reader ask, "Hmmmm, what is the answer to *that* question?"

You can use color to break-up the blocks of copy or highlight information.

2. The letter. Start with the "headline". The catch word to be printed in big letters or color.

The first paragraphs give you the complete message of the entire letter.

The first sentence: direct mail expert Ed McLean in a now classic opening sentence began with: "If the list on which we found your name is any indication . . ."

What was he doing? This: saying you are someone special and distinct and important.

That's enough to keep them reading . . .

Different paragraph indenting breaks up the page. Makes it more interesting to read.

End your letter with a signature (signed in blue) and a **P.S.** special offer (send money with order and receive free issues).

3. The brochure. Starting with the Ten Commandments, numbers make people stop and pay attention, and pique their curiosity for finding out more. Inside list one-sentence, tantalizing summaries of stories or articles recently run.

The publisher's letter. This little fold-over piece of paper adds less than a penny to the cost of your package and means an automatic increase in replies. The name "publisher's letter" first came about because it was used by book publishers to give you one more reason you should buy their books. The opening line is always similar to this one: "DON'T BOTHER TO READ THIS unless you're not sure about accepting the proposal" with someone's name or initials inside. There is one more reason to buy given by an officer of the company or well-known person.

4. The order blank. This is a summary of everything you have put in your letter. Here you can pick up the *free* offer and make it a tear-off piece on the end of the Business Reply Card. A headline could be helpful here.

Repeat the "extra" benefit on the order blank. Example: Two free issues if they send in check with order.

Remember:: Your order blank is your last-minute salesman.

So tell your reader exactly what to do. Be specific. Give specific instructions on mailing the reply card or using an 800 number. If you've included an involvement device, say how to punch out the token or remove the label and where to place it before responding.

Describe exactly how you want the reply card filled And tell the reader to "cut along this line" and "print your name here' and "put stamp here . . ."

5. *The business reply envelope.* All they have to do now is check what they want on the order blank, tuck it into the envelope and toss it in the nearest mailbox. No writing. No stamp-putting-on. They make it easy for you . . .

TOOLBOX

If you want to find out what kind of letters *really* work, the best way to show you is those that did and do.

The following pages are reprints of actual successful letters. We have included explanations on the purposes they were trying to achieve and the techniques they use.

Types of Letters

Up until now, you probably thought a letter was a letter.

Not really. There are many different ways to write your letter to make it different, unique, stand out and in front of all the other letters received in the morning mail.

Here are examples of letters that worked for us and others. Ideas you could adapt and adopt for yourself.

No one style of letter works all the time for everyone. But some style of letter works sometime for someone. Best way to find out: try some of the different formats shown on the following pages. You will find out very quickly certain letters are too "gimmicky" or "artificial" for you. When you copy some of the following styles, *your own style* will soon emerge—a format which is comfortable, easy and believable to you. And—more important—to your customer.

The Marketing to Your Market Letter

The first rule of any kind of advertising is to remember it is far, far easier to sell more to the customer you have than to sell a new customer. This is an axiom that is made for direct marketing.

The following three letters prove that point.

1. The Bank Letter. The problem: a small bank was losing money in

New York City. How could he compete with the giants? He decided to contact just the people in his community, which was only a small part of New York City.

2. *The Insurance Letter.* The problem: insurance companies all came out with a new low-premium policy for non smokers. How could this one agent let his non smoking customers become aware of this new low premium before they went to another company?

3. *The Supermarket Letter.* The problem: how to contact the new people who move into a community and have them buy groceries from you? If one out of five people moves every year, is there a way to contact the new people?

The Bank Letter

The bank was one of the smallest in New York City, and it wanted to increase its deposits. Chelsea National Bank president Merton Corn knew what he could not do. He could not afford to advertise on TV. He could not afford to advertise in *The New York Times*. He could not afford to advertise on the New York City radio stations top-rated drive time. He could not afford to advertise in the magazines in New York City. However, he could afford direct mail.

He drew a circle around his bank located just below Central Park in Manhattan. He said this "community" within the circle was the "city" where his bank was located. Then he began his direct marketing advertising campaign.

He put together a series of letters, each aimed at a different market.

- Firefighters and police officers received letters at their station or precinct houses. Their checks were issued twice a month. Why take them home? Why not simply deposit them in the nearby Chelsea Bank? Corn knew that the main reason people choose a particular bank is convenience. He would take this advantage and make it work for him.

- Current depositors received letters offering incentives if they opened additional accounts with the bank. If you had a minimum savings account, you also could have "free checking." The more accounts customers have with a bank, the less likely they are to switch banks. If a customer has a savings account, the odds are 2 to 1 he or she will not leave before the end of the year. If the customer has a checking and savings account, the odds jump to 10 to 1; if the customer has three accounts, the odds are 25 to 1. If the customer has four accounts, the odds go to 100 to 1. Corn wanted not only

Dear

I want to offer you a better banking deal than I think you have now
because we are a small bank, located nearby; we are anxious to attract
depositors such as yourself.

We have the following things to offer which we think will be of interest
to you:

1. No-charge checking accounts if you maintain a $500 savings account
    with us. We pay the maximum interest rate allowed by law for
    commercial banks from day of deposit to day of withdrawal.

2. Long hours - 8:30 a.m. to 5:00 p.m., Monday through Friday.

3. We have special free checking accounts for senior citizens.

4. We would be happy to arrange with the Department of Health, Education
    and Welfare; Social Security Administration, for direct deposit of
    any social security checks to our bank, saving you time and effort
    in making deposits.

5. We have a large supply of safe deposit boxes in which to store your
    valuables.

I am enclosing signature cards for savings and checking accounts and a postage
paid envelope for your convenience. If you prefer, stop in and say hello to
our Branch Manager.

                              Sincerely yours,

                              President

P.S. If you have any questions, please do not hesitate to call me.

Telling the Neighbors Who You Are

to attract new depositors, but also to increase the accounts held by current customers.

- Corporate personal accounts. Corn wrote letters to companies that borrowed from the bank for their businesses, asking if they would also like to have a personal account in the bank. At the end of this letter, he added the postscript (the best read part of any letter): "We will, of course, try to show our appreciation for this expression of confidence in us." If you were borrowing large sums of money for your business and the president of the bank wrote you asking for a personal account, would you oblige? How fast?

- President to president, Corn wrote the small businesses in his newly formed "circle city." His opening line was, "You're the president of a small business. I'm the president of a small bank. Why don't we get together and talk president to president." The implication was that the small business person might have a difficult time if he or she called Chase Manhattann and wanted to talk about business problems with David Rockefeller. But there **was** a bank president, Merton Corn, ready and willing.

This last letter campaign attracted so much attention that the headline was picked up and used by competitive banks as a way to increase their corporate business. Business jumped at the Chelsea Bank in both dollars and customers, all because of an advertising campaign that was limited to direct marketing.

The Insurance Letter

Jerry Rimm sells insurance in southern New Jersey. As an independent agent, he has a limited advertising budget.

One of his firms, Philadelphia Life Insurance Company, came out with a new policy for non smokers. The premiums were reduced drastically. A non smoker could nearly double the insurance coverage at about the same price. The company's brochure was full of facts, figures, and numbers. It was nearly impossible to read. "How many customers do you have under the letter A you think can use this new policy?" we asked.

"About thirty or so," said Rimm.

"Would you spend $10 on a direct mail campaign?"

"Ten dollars? Sure!"

He then mailed the thirty customers a letter. The outside of the envelope said, "For you—a non smoker." Inside, he enclosed the fact-filled, data-packed brochure from the insurance company. He also attached a small handwritten note personalized for each of the thirty customers. It said:

Dear (customer's name):

Now for the first time you, as a nonsmoker, can have $100,000 of life insurance for only $514 ($500,000 for $2,000).

The enclosed folder has the facts and figures. Call me today at 555-5201.

Jerry

Note the personalization from the name to the specific amount (because Rimm knew the customer's age) and the add-on suggested sale for the increased coverage. Within 72 hours, he sold more than $2 million of life insurance.

Ben Feldman's Story

There are more than 1,600 life insurance companies in America. Ben Feldman is one of the nation's top salesmen. By himself, he has written more insurance than 1,000 of the companies! He was the first insurance salesman to pass the goal of $25 million in one year.

And then doubled that figure.

Ben has been the leading salesman for New York Life for more than two decades. And he has set these records in a little town on the Ohio River: East Liverpool—a population about 20,000.

What is the secret of his success?

"Three things," says Ben.

"1. Work hard.

"2. Think big.

"3. Listen very well."

How he parlays each of these goals into million-dollar sales would take several chapters to describe. But he does use one indispensable marketing tool that helps him attain and exceed his own records: direct mail letters.

His letters are short, to the point and immediately visible. Here's an example:

Dear _____,

Will you trade one hour of your time for $1.00 each day for the rest of your life?

On July 14th, your insurance rates go up $1.00 per day forever.

Best wishes.

Ben Feldman.

The dates are from a private "birthday book" he keeps on his customers.

Once a month he mails out about twenty of these letters with a brand new dollar bill pinned to each one.

Results: "These letters result in policies of six and sometimes seven figures."

The Supermarket Letter

If you are newly married, or moving to rural southwestern Wisconsin, the odds are you will food shop at Dick's supermarkets.

The 31-year-old, five-store supermarket chain captures the major share of the retail food dollars in their market with—direct mail.

Their mail promotion began about twelve years ago, says President William Brodbeck, and it is still going strong.

Here's how it works:

1. The Lists. Store personnel put together three lists daily:

The newly arrived: who just moved into any shopping area with a Dick's supermarket. These names come from utilities, chambers of commerce, newspapers, and personal knowledge.

The newly married: Names culled from the society pages of the area newspapers.

The newly born: from birth announcements.

2. The Letters. The first two groups receive a letter from the manager of their nearest Dick's supermarket. He welcomes them to the community. He tells about Dick's. He lists the benefits and special features of his store.

3. The Offer. Included with each letter are six different coupons. Each is good for one free food item. One coupon redeemable each week for six consecutive weeks.

The coupons are for necessary merchandise: a five-pound bag of Idaho potatoes, a pound of cottage cheese, a dozen eggs, a half gallon of milk. All free.

4. The Next Letter. Bill Brodbeck writes a follow-up note about three weeks later, as President of Dick's. (How does he know they came? He doesn't bother to check since **90 percent of all mailed coupons were used!**)

He asks these new buyers a favor. Since they are now customers of Dick's, they can help the store do an even better job by simply answering the questions in the enclosed questionnaire, with a stamped, self-addressed envelope.

And, oh yes, for taking the time to answer the questionnaire, Dick's has included for you another six free food coupons to use, one a week for the next six weeks.

5. The Follow-Up. One year later this "new" customer has become a "steady" customer. Time for a new questionnaire based on the customer's experience with the store over the year. A follow-up file tells the Dick's secretary when the year has gone by. For taking the time to answer the questions, Dick's has enclosed for you a coupon for free goods at their bakery department.

6. *The Results:* Customers feel they are part of the Dick's family. The communities where Dick's stores are located are all small (population varies from 2,400 to 9,500). Everyone knows everyone. And everyone knows, respects and simply likes to shop at Dick's.

Customers also see their comments on the questionnaires put into action. ("We get back more than 85 percent of the questionnaires we send out," says Brodbeck. "And we read each one of them for ideas and suggestions.")

One repeated suggestion was a preference for bulk produce instead of pre-packaged. (Translation: you can pick and choose and hold and feel and examine each apple, orange, grape, tomato, instead of having them pre-packaged and pre-selected and pre-priced by the store.) Dick's switched to what the customers wanted. Sales increased!

The other value of the questionnaire: cross-selling. When a customer is asked an opinion on the photo finishing service or recipe cards ("Do you pick up our recipe cards each week?"), some never knew, until that moment, the store had photo finishing service and recipe cards. The questionnaire became a selling tool, a subconscious reminder "If this is what you want to buy, too, we have it, folks.")

The third mailer is the most recent in their promotion. This letter goes to the newborn babies. The names are sent to Dick's by local hospitals. This letter is addressed to the baby by name with a $2.00 coupon "for your parents to use" for any baby product from food to clothing to accessories.

One year later, the baby receives another letter with congratulations on his or her birthday and, ah, yes, a coupon for 25 percent off that first birthday cake from the bakery department.

When we asked what changes were made in the program in the decade since it began, Brodbeck answered, "Very few." "If Dick's opens a new department in a particular store, we add that information to the letter. But the copy has not changed. And the food items have not changed."

The original choice of giving away basic food items is as strong today as the day the first mailing went out. "We wanted items to have universal appeal with the highest usage. What worked when we first tried it still works today," Brodbeck says.

Remember: the letters, while not changing, are really new to the customer receiving them for the first time. To Dick's it is the same letter as mailed a decade ago. To the person receiving the letter, it is as fresh, interesting and up-to-date as the morning's newspaper.

Does Bill Brodbeck recommend this direct mail program for other food retailers? Yes! "It's an excellent way to encourage the customer to shop

DICK'S SUPER MARKETS' CUSTOMER QUESTIONNAIRE

Please help us help you by taking a few moments to place a checkmark
on the most appropriate line and by noting specific comments.

I most often shop at Dick's of _____ (City).

1. Dick's has a Meat De_____ that is ___ 'Poor, ___ Fair, ___ Good,
   ___ Very Good, ___ _____ause:

   _____   _____

   _____   _____

2. Dick's has a P_____ ___ ir, ___ Good,
   ___ Very Good, ___

   _____   _____

   _____   _____

3. Dick's has _____ Good,
   ___ Very Go_____

   _____   _____

   _____

4. Dick's has a _____ ___ Poor, ___ Fair,
   ___ Good, ___

   _____

   _____

5. Dick's has a De_____ ___od,
   ___ Very Good, ___

   _____

   _____

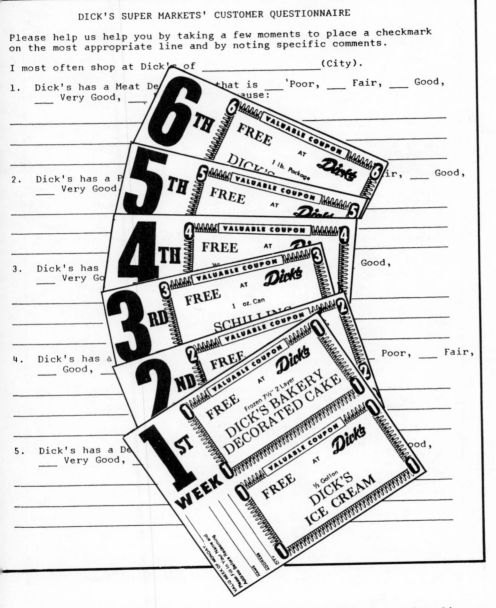

If You Move to Wisconsin and you are near a Dick's supermarket, this
is the letter you will receive from the manager. He includes six coupons
for two free food items for six consecutive weeks to use in his store.

October 9, 1984

Mr. & Mrs. John Jones
220 West Pine Street
Platteville, WI 53818

Dear Mr. & Mrs. Jones:

We are delighted to hear the good news of your recent marriage!
All the friendly personnel at DICK'S would like to add their
congratulations to your many others.

To help you begin this new phase of your life, we'd like to extend
a special invitation to visit our home owned super market. To
briefly acquaint you with DICK'S:

1. Our meat department features meats with "T.V.T." --
    Top Value Trim, trimmed at our market, not your table. . .
    for proven better meat value. Choose between Dick's and
    Lean and Tender and U.S. Choice Beef.

2. If you like salads, and who doesn't, our produce department
    boasts the largest selection of fresh fruits and vegetables
    around.

3. The best of "what comes naturally in Wisconsin," plus
    a complete frozen food, fowl, and fish selection is
    available in our dairy-frozen food department.

4. Our grocery department features the BEST in fine foods
    at DICK'S everyday low prices. Please compare; you'll
    find them lowest.

5. Our bakery contains home baked goodness of unexcelled
    quality and variety at reasonable prices.

We would enjoy serving you and showing you that it pays to shop
DICK'S where reasonable prices are always in effect. Enclosed you
will find six coupons which we hope you will use during the next
three weeks. Please bring them with you to our store and ask for
me, for I would appreciate the opportunity of meeting you.

Sincerely,

Store Manager

Dick's SUPER MARKETS

your store on multiple occasions. The value of the free coupons almost guarantees what will happen."

The trick of course is to catch the customer before he or she start a habit pattern by shopping a competitive store. Brodbeck adds, "By attracting these new customers to our store early. We have a great opportunity to convince them our store is *the* store they ought to shop."

A few years ago, addressing the Food Marketing Institute's national convention of thousands of retail food stores from all over the United States, Brodbeck talked about his store saying, "Our reputation rests on a very open relationship with our customers. We do our best to communicate with them often and in meaningful ways."

That basic philosophy is behind this very sucessful direct mail campaign. "Above all," he sums up, "we must keep the communications open with our customers."

This well-coordinated, thought-out and carefully followed-through direct mail program is a guide for any merchant in any businses. It is also a reminder that the customer not only has to be originally sought but must also be continually looked after and listened to.

A successful direct mail promotion that has not changed in two decades and still brings customers back and back and back and back and back.

The Headline Letter

We find this approach works well for us. Perhaps because we are print-oriented. We look for the appealing headline for an advertisement on the outside of the envelope. What group of words will capture the readers' interest and make them want to keep on reading?

Instead of using those words and/or phrases in the opening *sentence,* why not use them up there on top of the letter? All capital letters. Flush left. Or centered. Underlined. Double-spaced.

- *Eliminates a personal greeting.* You can type in the person's name, title, address as shown, but you do not have to repeat the name if you have a headline.
- *Sets the tone immediately.* The reader knows at once what the letter is all about. The whole concept is digested into the headline.
- *Gives you breathing room to write.* After you have captured the reader's interest with the headline, the customer will keep on reading to find out what the headline means. This means you can go into more detail about your merchandise/product/offer *before* explaining what the headline is all about.

the alley deli

Gordon's Alley. Atlantic City, N.J.
Established 1984. Proprietor: Norman Gordon
Take out & delivery service: 345-1060

Richard Squires, County Executive
1125 Atlantic Avenue
Atlantic City, New Jersey

WHOEVER SAID THERE'S NO SUCH THING AS A

FREE LUNCH DIDN'T KNOW ABOUT THIS LETTER.

Good morning.

Let me introduce myself.

My name is Norman Gordon. I own the just-opened Alley Deli in
Gordon's Alley.

And if you're wondering whatever happened to the good old-fashioned
(and delicious) deli sandwich...it's back. Right here!

I've enclosed a copy of our menu. And I'm so proud of the excellent
quality and superb taste of everything we have, I would like you to
be a charter member of our TASTER'S CLUB.

It's a great organization. No dues. No meetings. All you have to
do is eat and enjoy.

Your only requirement is to accept one free lunch from me.

Whoever said there's no such thing as a free lunch?

There is.

For you.

I'll call you in a few days. Pick and choose what you want from the
enclosed menu. And I'll have it delivered to you a short time after
I call.

Enjoy!

Norman Gordon.

Norman Gordon

RESULTS

ALLEY DELI

This letter was sent by a new small restaurant to influential people in the community: elected officials, prominent businessmen, professionals. Purpose: to build customers, make them aware the restaurant was open. Cost was minimal. For 100 letters, postage and typing—under $30.

Reaction was excellent. More than half took advantage of the free sandwich. And about half (25) ordered *at least one more* sandwich.

Within a month, 25 percent were steady come-in or call-up customers.

With a very, very small budget, the use of this letter achieved maximum results.

THE PRESIDENTIAL CARD (AUSTRALIA)

When we met Tony Ingleton of Melbourne, Australia, at the Pan Pacific Direct Marketing Symposium in Sydney in 1981, we were impressed with his new Presidential Card program. It offered members an opportunity to save money on hotel rooms, restaurant meals, rent-a-car and other expenses.

We examined his entire mailing program. We suggested new ways to promote not only his *new* membership but also how to re-activate members who did *not* renew. (See "Did I lose a letter from you . . .")

And so we wound up with all kinds of letters:

1. For new members.

2. For members who did not respond to the first request for renewal, a reminder letter.

3. For members who did not renew, a reason for renewing six months down the road.

Turn the page to see what happened.

Because of his letters . . .

1. Membership doubled.

2. Retention rate doubled. (Because the customer was contacted again if he did not respond the first time around . . .)

Today, more than 25,000 Australians belong to the Presidential Card with more signing up every day at a rate nearly double the rate of a few years ago. This success is due mainly to the letters since they are his major form of advertising.

The Tell-the-World Letter

You've seen this as an ad that usually begins, "An open letter to . . ." (Fills in the blank with the audience you are trying to reach.)

Melbourne Office: 6th Floor, Trak Centre,
445 Toorak Road, Toorak 3142
Telephone (03) 240 0727

Adelaide Office: Shop 3,
20 Hindmarsh Square, Adelaide 5000
Telephone (08) 223 1722, 223 1474

Tony Ingleton
President

HOW THE PRESIDENTIAL CARD
WAS RENAMED THE "MONEY SAVER"

When Robert Fisher of South Australia started his driving holiday, he was concerned whether or not he had enough money to last the trip.

On previous holidays the money he planned-to-spend was always exceeded by the money he spent. He was sure this time would not be different.

To his surprise, it <u>was</u> different. In fact, as he says, "I actually came home with money in my pocket because of my 'money saver'."

The "money saver" Robert Fisher wrote about is his <u>Presidential Card</u>. Here is what he said in his letter to us:

> "I have only just returned from a driving holiday
> through Queensland, New South Wales and Victoria.
> My Card was truly a great help and what a money
> saver. I actually came home with money in my
> pocket!"

Robert Fisher's letter is typical of those that arrive at our office every week thanking us for their "money saver" and the new places visited because they had, in their pocket, their personal <u>Presidential Card.</u>

As a cardholder, you enjoy dining at fine restaurants, staying at quality hotels, watching excellent entertainment. <u>That's why I am sending you your new money-saving Presidential Card membership, as your existing membership card expires in less than 30 days.</u> I want to make sure you keep on saving money, like V. W. Harding.

Mr Harding lives in South Australia. He wrote to us, "Since I began using my Card, I saved $330.00. That's nearly 1,000% profit on my original investment."

In addition - there's new exciting places to visit and a special bonus offer for you as a current member.

(Please turn for new places and bonus offer...)

E

Melbourne Office: 13th Floor, State Bank Building,
270 Flinders Street, Melbourne 3000
Telephone 63 8180 63 5523
Commercial Sales 63 8587

Adelaide Office: 12th Floor, Royal Insurance Building,
13 Grenfell Street, Adelaide 5000
Telephone (08) 212 5899 212 5651

Tony Ingleton
President

DID I LOSE A LETTER FROM YOU?

Every day the mailman delivers hundreds of letters to our Melbourne office.

Once in a while a letter is lost. Falls off the desk. Tucked into the wrong pile. Or . . . simply, not delivered.

And then someone will call us and ask, "Why didn't my Presidential Card arrive in the mail?" Or, "I wrote to you three weeks ago and I'm still waiting for my Presidential Card to come."

Frustration.

We can understand how that can happen with new members. (We can understand, but constantly upgrade our systems to minimise errors.)

But we are positively, absolutely, uncontrollably perplexed when it happens to a valued member of the past.

That's you.

THE REASON FOR OUR CONCERN: YOUR PRESIDENTIAL CARD EXPIRED AT THE END OF LAST MONTH AND WE DID NOT RECEIVE YOUR RENEWAL MEMBERSHIP FEE.

That happens, of course. There are vacations. There is the first-things-first approach where you deal with emergencies and must-do decisions at once. Everything else waits. Our concern is that sometime within the next few days you will go to the movies. Or dine at a favourite restaurant. Or be called away suddenly on a trip. And find yourself paying too much money for your entertainment, meal or hotel room.

The many reasons you joined The Presidential Card club in the beginning are still there. Only more so. Today there are more than 500 establishments that honour the Presidential Card throughout Australia. Your membership renewal lets you continue to save up to 50% off the regular price of hotel and motel rooms, restaurant meals, movie tickets, amusement centres, rental cars . . . and more.

You know from past experience your annual membership fee comes back to you the first few times you use your Presidential Card – (the ONLY travel and entertainment card that saves you money every time you use it).

As valuable as your Presidential Card was for you in the past, it becomes even more so in the future – with more places to go, visit, stay and dine.

Return the enclosed invoice with your cheque, thus enabling you to get full use of your renewal Presidential Card, which was forwarded to you at the beginning of last month.

Sincerely,

Tony Ingleton

TONY INGLETON
Club President

PS.   If someone told you the new membership rate increased to $40.00, they are correct. But as a re-subscriber, you may re-enroll for your last membership rate of only $35.00

PPS.   We've enclosed an order form and postage reply paid envelope, just to make sure your answer comes directly to us.

L 1

What it does: Takes the intimacy of a letter and captures *some* of the same personal relationship on a large scale. True, the letter is now written to everyone instead of someone but results can be dramatic.

Banks did this very effectively when Congress decided to tax your interest on savings by having banks withhold the taxes. Banks ran sample letters in newspapers all over America asking people to use these letters to write their Congressmen to repeal the law.

Millions wrote. The law was repealed. The mass letter worked.

Special interest groups use this same approach when they want you to communicate with a decision-maker. The back page of the Sunday *New York Times* often has a letter from one of these groups asking you to write in support of their cause.

This letter has the advantage of:

* *Mass audience.* You reach a lot of people . . . and quickly.
* *Massive response.* If you touch the right emotional response, the response can be overwhelming and immediate.

RESULTS

We first saw this letter from Sun Bank in Florida. We used it at a national bank marketing convention. The audience stood up and cheered when they saw it on the screen.

Within a few short months, small banks around the country picked up this ad and reported good reaction from their customers.

They knew they had to play catch-up ball because Congress gave them the tools to fight this new opposition late in the game. Showing the customer how to write a letter to take money *out* of brokerage houses and put it back into banks created an immediate and significant increase in deposits.

The Newsweek subscription letter. Nearly 107 million of these letters were mailed out by *Newsweek!*

The letter was written by direct mail expert Ed McLean. The next two pages tell you, in his words, the history behind the success of this letter.

One hint why it worked: Count the number of times he uses the word *"You."* It's at least 27 times on just this *first* page.

"It was the first direct mail piece I ever wrote," says Ed. "It was in 1960. When I came to work there old timers told me there was only one way to sell subscriptions to *Newsweek* and that was with colorful, expensive mailing pieces. I looked over what they did and knew why *I* never subscribed to *Newsweek.* The copy was full of slogans and claims, few of them with any supporting material.

"I read through several years of the magazine—a practice I still follow today when creating a subscription letter—and got a 'feel' for what the

How to tell your broker you're taking your money back to Sun Bank.

Date_____

Dear Merrill Lynch ☐
    Paine-Webber ☐
    E. F. Hutton ☐
    Shearson ☐
    Bache
    Others_____
    (Check One)

I'm taking my money out of your money market fund and depositing it into the new Sun Bank Money Market Account.

It's not that you didn't serve my needs. It's just that Sun Bank can now serve them much better.

Sun Bank pays money market rates just as you do. But my deposits are directly insured through the Federal Deposit Insurance Corporation. You can't offer that insurance. Sun Bank guarantees my weekly rate. You don't. And after opening my account, they don't limit the amount I can deposit or withdraw.

Plus, Sun Bank offers a whole range of banking services, like auto loans, safe deposit boxes, statewide 24-hour banking and more. You certainly don't have all those things to offer.

I guess what it boils down to, is that I'd rather do my banking with my bank.

Anyway, thanks for everything. It's a pity we never got to meet in person.

                        Sincerely,

                        (Sign Here)

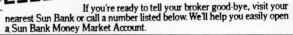

If you're ready to tell your broker good-bye, visit your nearest Sun Bank or call a number listed below. We'll help you easily open a Sun Bank Money Market Account.

Sun Bank

Begin with a story. That's what copywriter Ed McLean did in this letter for Xerox Learning Systems. Remember how Bill Jayme said he had to "become the reader"? McLean does the same thing here. A story opening is a good opening but only if it applies to the person receiving the letter.

Xerox Learning Systems
Depot Square
P.O. Box 825
Peterborough, NH 03458
(603) 924-9007

XEROX

Dear Executive:

Fresh out of college, he started at the financial services company as a management trainee at $200 a week.

That was nine years ago. Now, a string of promotions and several substantial salary increases later, he heads up one of the corporation's major profit centers, with over a hundred people under him.

A first-rate idea person, he looks for imaginative solutions to business challenges.

He gets in at nine, uses his time well, and rarely stays after five. At least one day a week he takes an early train home -- "to think and plan," he says.

His desk isn't always free of papers but it's cleared before he leaves. He's punctual, well-organized, effective in meetings. Yet those around him call him low-keyed, even a bit laid-back.

What's most important: at age 33 he feels good about himself, his job, his life, his future. By next year, if another firm hasn't made him an irresistible offer, he'll be ready for new and larger responsibilities within the company.

An unusual person? Not really. In my work I see many men and women in management who function as well as this man does.

My name is John J. Franco. I am President of a division of Xerox Corporation known as Xerox Learning Systems. Our business is helping people do a better job. We serve thousands of corporations, including 417 of the Fortune 500.

Recently, a number of our clients asked us to help them find out why some executives seem to handle their jobs with ease while others, just as bright and talented, must work harder and longer to achieve the same result.

In the process, unfortunately, many of these otherwise able

This letter helped sell 1,200 out-of-date diesel cars. The reader is immediately brought into a controversial discussion at the beginning of the letter. This letter won Ed McLean the Direct Marketing Association's Gold Mailbox award and documented a total of more than $6.5 million in sales of Mercedes diesels, SLs and other models.

(This is the beginning of an eight page letter! Does long copy sell?)

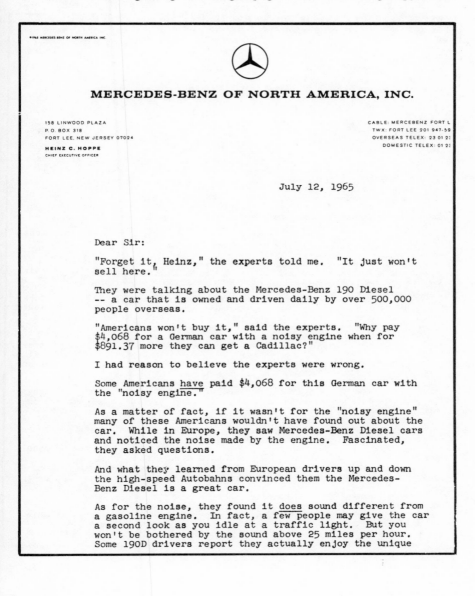

©1965 MERCEDES-BENZ OF NORTH AMERICA INC.

MERCEDES-BENZ OF NORTH AMERICA, INC.

158 LINWOOD PLAZA
P.O. BOX 318
FORT LEE, NEW JERSEY 07024

HEINZ C. HOPPE
CHIEF EXECUTIVE OFFICER

CABLE: MERCEBENZ FORT L
TWX: FORT LEE 201 947-59
OVERSEAS TELEX: 23 01 2!
DOMESTIC TELEX: 01 2!

July 12, 1965

Dear Sir:

"Forget it, Heinz," the experts told me. "It just won't sell here."

They were talking about the Mercedes-Benz 190 Diesel -- a car that is owned and driven daily by over 500,000 people overseas.

"Americans won't buy it," said the experts. "Why pay $4,068 for a German car with a noisy engine when for $891.37 more they can get a Cadillac?"

I had reason to believe the experts were wrong.

Some Americans <u>have</u> paid $4,068 for this German car with the "noisy engine."

As a matter of fact, if it wasn't for the "noisy engine" many of these Americans wouldn't have found out about the car. While in Europe, they saw Mercedes-Benz Diesel cars and noticed the noise made by the engine. Fascinated, they asked questions.

And what they learned from European drivers up and down the high-speed Autobahns convinced them the Mercedes-Benz Diesel is a great car.

As for the noise, they found it <u>does</u> sound different from a gasoline engine. In fact, a few people may give the car a second look as you idle at a traffic light. But you won't be bothered by the sound above 25 miles per hour. Some 190D drivers report they actually enjoy the unique

The Get-'em-Excited Letter. This letter screams, yells, cajoles and has all kinds of interesting colors and underlinings to make you wonder what's coming next. We've listed some of the many things going on in this letter.

ANOTHER MONEY-SAVING FEATURE -- REFILLS AT D.R.I. DISCOUNT PRICES!

It happens to everyone. A project takes so many fasteners of one type that even with this Shop you run low. No problem! No need to make a special trip to the hardware store and pay those high prices, either. We include a refill label with your Shop so you can order any type or size -- any time. And at our dollar-stretching discount prices, like these ...

4

SAVE EVEN MO on refills!

100 Machine Screws #6 - 32 x 1"   Average Retail $2.25   Our Price $.91

100 Internal Tooth Washers #6   Average Retail $1.21   Our Price $.29

Take advantage of this money-saving offer and I'll send you THREE VALUABLE FREE GIFTS! A wall-size Specifications Chart AND a Nut & Bolt Gauge (so you know exactly what type and size fastener to use) ... PLUS a Three Angle Level. All three are yours to keep, FREE. See the enclosed literature for details.

3

PLUS ... A MONEY-BACK GUARANTEE!

2

I really believe in our products. I also believe in going out of my way to make sure you're satisfied. That's why D.R.I. offers you a 100% money-back guarantee. If you're not pleased with your Shop, if it doesn't save you a lot of time and money, just return it. You'll get a full refund, including shipping and handling charges.

3

With a guarantee like this, you've nothing to lose, everything to gain. So take the time to order now. When you do, check your gift list. Chances are friends and relatives will appreciate this "hardware store" as much as you. (Check your order card -- you save even more when you order in quantity!)

Just fill in the enclosed Order Card and mail it with your check, money order or company purchase order for $19.99 plus $3.90 shipping and handling ... or charge it to your VISA, MasterCard, American Express, Diners Club or Carte Blanche account.

Remember, the demand for the Nut & Bolt Shop is heavy. Mail your order today ... I can't guarantee prompt delivery if you delay ordering.

Sincerely,

Stephen R. Zastera

Stephen R. Zastera
Vice President, General Manager

If you aren't 100% satisfied with your Shop, return it. You'll get a prompt full refund. I guarantee it. *4*

P.S. PLUS THIS SPECIAL BONUS OFFER!   *3*

Made in Taiwan

Here's another great value -- the 105-PIECE WALL ANCHOR SET! You get three different color coded sizes and 35 of each size: 35 for #4-6-8 self-tapping screws; 35 for 6-8-10 self-tapping screws; 35 for 10-12 self-tapping screws. Just the anchor you need for fastening in wood, plasterboard, brick, concrete, tile and much more. All organized in a handy plastic case.

It has a $4.79 retail value. But you can purchase the complete 105-Piece Set at our low price of $1.99 plus $.50 shipping and handling! Note: Wall Anchor Sets cannot be purchased separately.

---

1. Facsimile of handwriting to look as though it was a last minute thought. This is in contrasting blue ink. **2.** The parentheses and underscores in blue ink. **3.** The sentence "Here's more good news . . .", "But because . . .", "Everything you need" is highlighted in yellow. As well as the capitalized words and "with a guarantee . . ." P.S. offers yet ANOTHER value and first sentence in yellow. **4.** The handwritten items are in blue, including signature.

NEWSWEEK • 117 EAST THIRD STREET • DAYTON 2, OHIO

Dear Reader:

If the list upon which I found your name is any indication, this is not the first -- nor will it be the last -- subscription letter you receive. Quite frankly, your education and income set you apart from the general population and make you a highly-rated prospect for everything from magazines to mutual funds.

You've undoubtedly 'heard everything' by now in the way of promises and premiums. I won't try to top any of them.

Nor will I insult your intelligence.

If you subscribe to Newsweek, you won't get rich quick. You won't bowl over friends and business associates with clever remarks and sage comments after your first copy of Newsweek arrives. (Your conversation <u>will</u> benefit from a better understanding of the events and forces of our era, but that's all. Wit and wisdom are gifts no magazine can bestow.) And should you attain further professional or business success during the term of your subscription, you'll have your own native ability and good luck to thank for it -- not Newsweek.

What, then, can Newsweek do for <u>you</u>?

The answer depends upon what type of person you happen to be. If you are not curious about what's going on outside your own immediate daily range of concern...if you are quickly bored when the topic of conversation shifts from <u>your</u> house, <u>your</u> car, <u>your</u> ambitions...if you couldn't care less about what's happening in Washington or Wall Street, in London or Moscow...then forget Newsweek. It can't do a thing for you.

If, on the other hand, you are the kind of individual who

would like to keep up with national and international affairs,
space and nuclear science, the arts -- but cannot spend hours
at it...if you're genuinely interested in what's going on with
other members of the human race...if you recognize the big stake
you have in decisions made in Washington and Wall Street, in
London and Moscow...

    then Newsweek may well be the smartest investment you
could make in the vital weeks and months ahead!

    For little more than 1¢ a day, as a Newsweek subscriber,
your interest in national and international affairs will be served
by over 200 top-notch reporters here and around the world. Each
week, you'll read the most significant facts taken from their
daily dispatches by Newsweek's editors.

    You'll get the facts. No bias. No slanting.
    Newsweek respects your right to form your own
    opinion.

In the eventful weeks to come, you'll read about

    -election strategy (Who will run against JFK? Medicare,
      education, unemployment: how will they sway voters?)

    -Administration moves (New civil-rights bill in the
      works? Taxes: what next?)

    -G.O.P. plans (Stepped-up activity in Dixie? New faces
      for Congressional races?)

    -Kremlin maneuverings (Will Cold War policies change?
      New clashes with Red China?)

    -Europe's future (New leaders, new programs? How can
      America compete with the Common Market?)

You'll also keep on top of latest developments in the exciting
fields of space and nuclear science. Whether the story describes
a space-dog's trip to Venus or the opening of a new area in the
peaceful use of atomic fission, you'll learn the key facts in
Newsweek's Space & The Atom feature -- the first and only weekly
department devoted to space and nuclear science in any newsweekly.

    The fascinating world of art will be reviewed and interviewed
for you in Newsweek. Whether you are interested in books or

ballet, painting or plays, movies or music -- or all of them -- you will find it covered fully and fairly in Newsweek.

Subscribe now and you'll read about

international film awards...new art shows at the Louvre in Paris...the opening of the Metropolitan and La Scala opera seasons...glittering first nights on and off Broadway...plus revealing interviews with famed authors and prima donnas, actors and symphony conductors.

AND you'll be briefed on happenings in the worlds of Business and Labor (More wage demands now?)...Education and Religion (Reforms in teacher training? More church mergers?)...Science and Medicine (Cancer, arthritis cures on the way?)...Sports and TV-Radio (New world records? More educational TV, fewer MD shows?)

You read Newsweek at your own pace. Its handy Top of the Week index lets you scan the top news stories of the week in two minutes. When you have a lull in your busy schedule, you can return to the story itself for full details. In this way, you are assured of an understanding of the events and forces of our era.

TRY Newsweek.

Try it at our special introductory offer:

37 WEEKS OF NEWSWEEK FOR ONLY $2.97

That's about 8¢ a week -- little more than a penny a day. You would pay $9.25 at newsstands for the same number of copies; $4.98 at our regular yearly subscription rates.

And try it with this guarantee: if, after examining several issues in your own home, you do not agree that Newsweek satisfies your news interests, you will receive a prompt refund.

An order form is enclosed, along with a postage-paid return envelope. Do initial and return the order form today. We'll bill you later, if you wish.

Sincerely,

S. Arthur Dembner

S. Arthur Dembner
Circulation Director

SAD/jnb

editors were trying to do. I had been a salesman, selling door to door and I always tried to catch the housewife's attention and interest quickly. If I didn't, I would fail.

"Applying this to *Newsweek* subscription direct mail, I set out to capture the reader's attention in the first paragraph. As someone new to direct mail, I was curious about mailing lists and I suspected other people were, too. So I started in what I thought was a straightforward manner, acknowledging the fact that we had found the reader's name on a mailing list of affluent people.

"Then I sold the value of being well informed, which is a key benefit. And this led to a discussion of some features which *Newsweek* would likely cover. I sensed that people subscribed to a newsmagazine for the future, not for the present or past. And I found out that this was so: trial subscriptions to *Time* and *Newsweek* are easier to sell just before a national election or other major event.

"The letter cost less than one-half of what the control cost and produced twice as many orders.

"This letter was the *Newsweek* control through the Sixties and well into the Seventies, until a free calculator offer beat it. I have been told that nearly 107 million copies of the letter were mailed before it was retired."

Please Fold, Tear, Spindle, Staple or Mutilate

The next time you go use the mail for sales, try stapling, pinning or clipping an attachment to your letter. Try attaching a note and/or change the color of the paper or ink. Try an unusual fold that produces a progressive disclosure technique—you read only small parts of the copy with each fold. Other folds can simulate the opening of curtains, doors or windows. Fan folds are always attention getters. Use your imagination. Chances are that your competitor could care less about how *his* mailing is folded.

We even mutilated a mailing to attract attention. For a fund-raising letter, we actually had part of the mailing burned. (Yes, there are suppliers who will scorch or burn the edges of your mailing piece.)

Inexpensive slitting or die cuts have unlimited possibilities. In a mailing for a Columbus Day Sale, we put a slit in a picture of a bottle floating in the ocean. Stuffed in the slit was a separate note which could be pulled out of the bottle.

The P.S. is at the . . . beginning of the letter? Since it is a well-known fact that the P.S. is one of the best-read parts of a letter, this one *begins* with the P.S.

A certain attention-grabber, this P.S. explains why it is placed at the beginning, follows that with a major benefit and follows that by . . . the *beginning* of the letter.

Esquire
Man At His Best

P.S. I realize that putting a 'P.S.' before the start of a letter is unorthodox, but I want you to know now -- at the beginning -- what will happen after you return the R.S.V.P. card...

First, you'll be able to subscribe to ESQUIRE at a remarkable savings: 67% below the regular cover price. Yes, 67% off.

In addition, as a subscriber, you'll receive a limited edition copy of "The Master Host: Esquire's Guide to Home Entertaining and Party Planning" -- completely FREE of cost, just as soon as we receive your payment.

What's more, you'll receive this special guarantee... if you ever decide that ESQUIRE is not for you, simply notify us, and we'll refund your money on all unmailed issues. No questions asked.

And that's what will happen later, if you mail your R.S.V.P. card now.

Dear Reader,

Are you headed for success? Are you <u>aiming</u> for it?

Will you know it when you find it? Could you use a good "road map"?

Rest assured, there <u>is</u> a road map to success. A timely,

Two Park Avenue   New York, New York 10016

The publisher's letter. We told you about it in chapter 7, I'm Going to Sit Right Down and Write Myself a Letter.

Each of these are fold-over pieces with a message similar to the one shown above. The readers are told they may read this note only if they decide *not* to buy.

The cost of these is only a penny or less (defending on quanities mailed) but they invariably increase sales so are worth the small added expense.

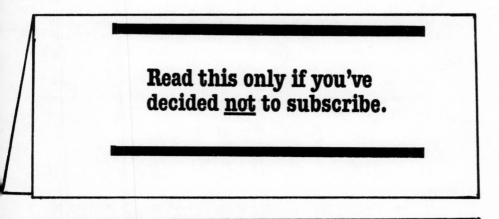

Read this only if you've decided not to subscribe.

From the desk of HENRY EARP Editorial Manager

Dear Reader:

In about 2400 carefully-chosen words every Monday The Kiplinger Washington Letter tells you what to plan for in the weeks and months ahead.

These 2400 words are the end-product of hundreds of thousands assembled through painstaking research and one-on-one interviews by me and 25 other Kiplinger editors. We spend the previous week buttonholing government and business leaders . . . analyzing every business forecast, economic report and statistical abstract we can lay hands on . . . so you won't have to.

Austin Kiplinger runs the shop . . . directs and edits the Letters. He is a former San Francisco & Chicago newsman, columnist and network commentator. (His father started the Letters back in 1923 to save time for busy executives by briefing them each week on business trends and government moves likely to affect business.)

With the accelerated pace of life . . . the enormous time pressures on executives . . . I don't have to tell you how much greater the need is today for consistently-accurate, concisely-presented business intelligence.

I hope you will accept our invitation to judge for yourself how well we are meeting that need – and how valuable we can be to you.

Sincerely,

Henry A. Earp

Editorial Manager

"Flashers" Attract Attention

We've been stumped! For a long time we've been trying to find a word, just the right word, to describe all of the little graphic nuances that can make a direct mail letter more effective. Now we think we have found that word. It's "flashers." Flashers seems the right word because flashers of any kind attract attention—and that's what we want them to do in our direct mail letters.

One of our favorite flashers is underlining, a way of calling attention to key points. Straight underlining has been popular since the beginning of direct mail and mail-order copywriting, but now there is a new approach—highlighting with color, just as students do in textbooks. It's a simple printing procedure that adds only one additional color to the printed piece.

Indenting is an often overlooked copy technique. It is particularly appropriate when you want to:

1. List features or benefits.
2. Sub-paragraph.
3. Break up long copy.

Some copywriters routinely indent copy on every page to insure easier reading.

Brackets may be the least used of the various flashers but they offer a change of pace.

Don't overlook handwritten notes . . . they really work! Handwritten notes tend not only to attract attention but also lend a personal touch to copy. Care should be taken to insure that the handwriting is completely legible.

Using lines to completely box-in portions of your letter is another version of the brackets technique but is usually reserved for special offers, conditions, guarantees or instructions. The box is most often used in combination with indentation.

Simulated rubber stamp impressions find applications for such things as calling attention to expiration dates of your direct mail offers.

Check marks, bullets and parentheses can also be used to break up long copy, as they help to keep the reader's attention.

Using a different color for any of our flashers adds to their effectiveness and makes for a more graphically pleasing letter. The most popular alternate colors are blue and red.

For a good example of the use of flashers, go back to our **get-'em-excited** letter.

8
Your Future Is in the Cards!

O UR PREFERRED CUSTOMERS receive postcards from us when we travel. Not the usual "wish you were here" but a selling message or an explanation of why we are *there*.

Most times we arrange to have a few dozen cards sent to us ahead of time with scenes indigenous to the country we are going to visit. We write and address the cards *before* we leave, take them with us and mail them from the country when we arrive.

Or we take pretyped name and address peel-off labels, buy the appropriate cards and every day write ten or more cards telling our best customers that we are thinking of them *wherever* we are.

We have written from Australia and Helsinki and London and Paris and Stockholm and Singapore and Hong Kong and Copenhagen.

We have written from the Grand Canyon and Yellowstone and Denver and Disneyland and New Orleans and Chicago and Boston and New York City.

These postcards carry a sales message but with the impact of an intimate person-to-person contact from a far-off place. And when we get back home, people actually thank us for sending them direct mail!

The postcard may be one of direct mail's most neglected techniques. Too frequently we overlook its many advantages, its versatility and the countless opportunities for its use.

Postcards are inexpensive.

They can be printed with any color ink, combinations of colors, on different color stock or in full color.

They can be designed in many sizes and shapes.

They can carry something other than the message. (More about this later.)

They require a minimum amount of copy or graphics.

111

And above all, (probably because of their "greetings" origin), postcards enjoy a very personal image.

Almost any marketing program can take advantage of postcards. Use picture postcards for new product introductions, particularly for products inconvenient for a salesperson to carry. Use postcards to announce a sale. (Big postcard for big sales?)

Use postcards to introduce a new salesman in a territory with his picture on one side of the card and a short "bio" on the other side.

Use postcards to build traffic at meetings, seminars and trade shows.

Postcards are a quick way to call attention to an address or telephone number change. An accounting service in Hawaii sends out a combined New Year's card and tax season message—and receives about a 15 percent *client* return!

We recently received a full color card with a picture of a crocus peeking out of the snow. The card was mailed from Breck in Holland announcing their annual tulip bulb sale.

Ray Jutkins, the popular writer/speaker of Nelson, Pandullo, Jutkins Direct Marketing, Inc. in California, sends friends and clients a picture postcard from his travels. Example: A picture of Mount Everest sent from Kathmandu when he was on his way to speak at a sales meeting in Manila. The back of the large postcard had a printed message telling of the meeting, a handwritten note from Ray, his picture and at the bottom—his company name, address and services offered.

Our favorite postcard story: There's a family who live in the pine forest of southern New Jersey on the road to the popular seashore resorts. During the winter, they scrawl notes on postcards offering free pickup of unwanted major appliances. These are mailed to a taxpayers list of vacation homeowners. Many part time residents decide to buy new appliances when they arrive at their summer homes but find it difficult to get rid of the old refrigerators and stoves. The note-writer comes in with his truck, picks up the old appliances and takes them to an open area in the woods facing one of the major highways leading to the resort.

His hand-painted FOR SALE sign attracts those who own rental units at the seashore. After a long, cold winter, they often have to replace inexpensive appliances for their tenants. Here's a successful small business, started by someone who uses a simple postcard to bring in, free, the products he sells.

Postcards are not restricted to one-way messages. They can be used as order cards to be filled in and returned in an envelope. Or as folded business reply cards. And for something really creative, *Penthouse* magazine attached a letter in an envelope to a giant postcard and gained the best of both worlds:

They had the impact of the picture postcard along with the long copy and order form included in the attached envelope.

Recently a company came up with a postcard that contains a peel-off self-adhesive sticker that can be used as a miniature bumper sticker or label.

Another company perforates a picture postcard in the shape of the standard Rotary telephone index. When torn from the postcard, the card contains a portion of the picture from the postcard on one side and the printed name, address and phone information on the reverse side. It's a unique way to get your name and message onto someone's desk file.

Postcards: an easy, simple and uncomplicated way for you to begin doing your direct mail.

Just sit down at your desk, pre-select some of your best customers and drop them a note about what you have for them that's new or on sale, or simply say you are thinking of them. (Few people do *that.*)

Postcards have come a long way since they were introduced in Austria in 1869 as straw-colored pieces of board called Korrespondenz Karte.

But they still perform the same service: telling someone else you were thinking of them and took the time to write and say so.

If what you want to say, offer or sell takes up more room than available on a postcard, it's time to move up to the next generation—the self-mailer. No envelope to open. Just unfold once or several times and read all about it . . .

The Bare Facts: Direct Mail Uncovered

Our New Year's Winter Sale direct mail pieces have been the same size, shape and look for the past fifteen years. And each one brings in more business that one day than we do most other *weeks* of the year.

We bring this to your attention at this point to emphasize the importance of self-mailers. They go it alone. And are very effective.

Look through your morning mail. Most are self-mailers. That means they are complete unto themselves. No envelope and brochure and special insert. What you see is what you get.

Postcards are one example. But there the message is out for everyone to see.

Self-mailers are most often folded with the message *inside,* and you open, turn, unfold to read because the headline makes you open, turn or unfold to read.

Self-mailers are typically folders, booklets, brochures, newsletters, circulars and catalogs.

Here's the advantage of self-mailers:

1. They are less expensive. (No envelope costs.)

2. They are easy to open. (No ripping of an envelope.)

3. They are easy to read. (The headline makes you open the first fold which makes you interested enough to unfold the next fold which . . .)

4. You can use the same address for going to the customer and coming *back* to you (See examples at end of this chapter.)

5. The response device (that means an order card or business reply card) is right there in front of you. Just check off what you want.

Here's the disadvantages of self-mailers:

1. Limited space for a detailed story or offer.

2. It says, "Hi there, folks. I'm an advertisement!" Which *can* be an advantage. For if the customer *knows* what it is and you have interested them enough to open and read, you are halfway home.

Here's some examples of self-mailers we all receive:

• *Marketing the Market.* You are the proud owner of a new expensive computer. You promptly fill in and mail your registration/guarantee card. Your name is sold as part of a mailing list of computer owners to a computer magazine. They send you a self-mailer. The teaser copy on the front says, "Congratulations! Your new [brand name] computer opens a wide world of information to you. And [name of magazine] helps you explore this exciting new world." The back of the self-mailer is filled with covers of recent issues of the magazine. Without opening an envelope . . . without removing a staple . . . without breaking a seal, you find tantalizing copy and graphics with just a simple unfolding. Right audience. Right offer. Right format.

• *Trading Up to the Trade.* "Coming to Philadelphia for the first time —a seminar for Manufacturers' Representatives" reads the teaser copy.

The back of this self-mailer lists the contents of the seminar (reasons for coming). The first inside panel has a personal message (in letter form) from the sponsor, a well-known authority on the subject. Another panel contains photographs and biographies of the speakers. Still one more panel has its testimonials from attendees in other cities. And finally—the panel with a registration form.

Effective?

Yes, which is why this is a standard format bringing thousands of attendees to conferences and seminars all over the country.

• *Food for Thought.* Ever stand in line in a supermarket behind someone with a whole fist full of coupons? Where did all those coupons come from? Many were part of a circular sent as a self-mailer to the many people with the same last name, "Occupant."

It seems every couple of weeks an alumnae bulletin comes from a college someone in our family attended. The one on our desk tonight is from Cedarcrest College, a women's college in Allentown, Pennsylvania. On the front is a picture of a student in a costume from the hit Broadway show

Cats. It's really eye-catching. The back side, under the indicia and address features a cover story concerning the student actress. And somewhere, somehow there is the real or implied request for contributions. Yes, in a self-mailer.

• *Mail Sail.* Ken is an ardent boater. His late August mail brings him an abbreviated catalog from his favorite marine supply house. See the bold headlines announcing end-of-season closeouts! Read all about the marvelous products you wanted to buy but could never afford. Now . . . buy!

No envelope to open. No putting it aside to find out (too late) what's inside. Everything is out front, bare, pictures, prices, and the convenience of a telephone call to make Ken's boat the best looking boat on the bay.

The main point: remember that mail is a many splendored thing. There are all kinds of ways to capture the customer's attention and have them read, re-read and re-act.

Not the least of which is to simply let it all hang out.

TOOLBOX

We were in Melbourne, Australia, talking to a group of life insurance agents from Australian Mutual Provident Society (AMP). We told them the importance of sending cards and showed a slide of the card below from insurance salesman Jack Wardlaw we receive every year on our birthday.

Suddenly someone in the audience stood and said, "I get one, too!" It seems he met Jack Wardlaw on a cruise.

Excited by this news, we repeated the story the next day in Brisbane and received a shock when *another* salesman in the back of the room yelled out, "And I get one from Jack every year too. I met him at the Million Dollar Round Table meeting in New Orleans!"

We called Jack when we returned. Down in Raleigh, eighty years young, still selling insurance ("And I can play the banjo as fast as the eye can see . . .")

How many cards did he mail every year? Well, he's been cutting back. Only mailing 15,000 a year now. Used to be 40,000. And all he does is sell and sell and sell and sell . . . (And did you notice above the birthday greeting a message on buying his book and cassette?)

JACK WARDLAW
For Life

P. O. Box 2121 - Telephone (919) 832-4433
Raleigh, North Carolina 27602
THE WARDLAW BUILDING
2008 Hillsborough Street

FORWARD AND RETURN POSTAGE GUARANTEE
ADDRESS CORRECTION REQUESTED

Have you read Jack Wardlaw' s book:
"Top Secrets of Successful Selling"?

Have you heard Jack Wardlaw's cassette:
"Thought Plus Action"?

If I should suddenly have to stop sending birthday greetings, I would still be thinking about you on your day!
. . . Jack

If It Says "Sale" and Looks Like a "Sale" Then It Must Be a . . .
This mailer was a giant sales ticket (4 inches wide by 8 inches long). You knew as soon as you looked at this piece that it was a sale because it *looked like* a sale.

When you opened this self-mailer, it unfolded to show all the items from the various shops on sale.

A strong, effective and results-achieving self-mailer.

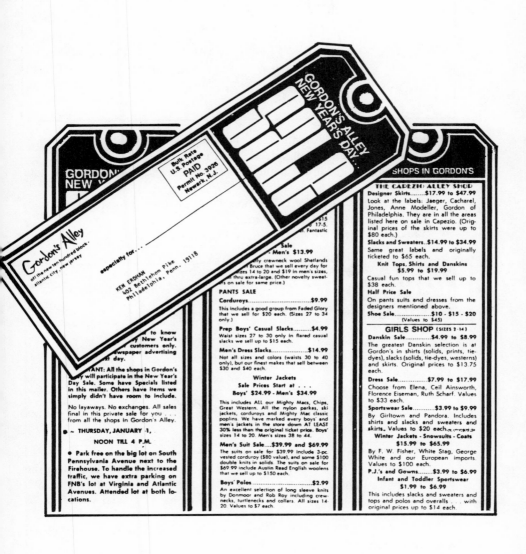

Frank Siracusa in Atlantic City, New Jersey, has these postcards pre-printed and mails them to all potential customers.

Notice how he fills in the name of the business and adds a personal note at the time.

We were impressed. We called him. "Sell us some insurance," we said. "Great," he answered, "what kind?"

"We don't know," we said, "we just like the card!"

The Mailer Is a . . . Check! Right. This is a mailing we sent with the person's name right up there in *front* on a *check!* When you opened this mailer it had a list of items in the store on sale for you (and your first 76 cents was free.)

The mailer was printed on *check paper* so it had a look of a real check when received in the mail by the customer.

A Monopoly Game Where Everyone Wins. This self-mailer opened up to a full newspaper-page size (above). But it folded down to a typewriter sheet of paper to go through the mails. Not only was the game familiar to the reader but it had the extra benefit of Monopoly originally coming from the same city as the store: Atlantic City.

Self-Mailers & Styles & Folds

Here are some examples of the most often seen-through-the-mails self-mailers. The designs and folds are limited only to your imagination, printer's capabilities and specific Post Office regulations. We've given them names (our own) and short descriptions of what they are and how they work.

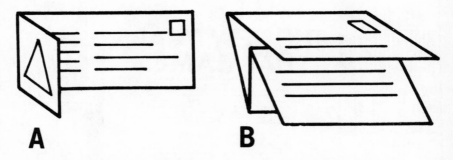

A   **B**

A. *The Corner Fold:* Only a part of the card is folded. Make sure the copy on the card exposed reads by itself. When the fold-over piece is laid flat you should still be able to read the entire message. Not half sentences or parts of words.

B. *The Tuck-In-And-Over:* This gives you a chance to capture the reader's interest as soon as the card is lifted. And/or a good spot to say, *"Stop!* How many of these questions can you answer?" And it becomes the back of a reply card where you have the customer now involved.

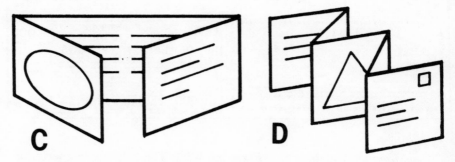

C   **D**

C. *The Split Definitive.* Gives you a big panorama look across all three folds when it opens.

D. *The Accordian Fold.* Good for providing enough room when you have several stories to tell. Each one has its own space.

E. *Tuck In & Over:* Good layout for lots of copy. Also serves well as a business reply envelope for one part and a message for the other.

F. *The Side Arm:* When you open this one, the narrow side piece should be a different color to announce an important feature.

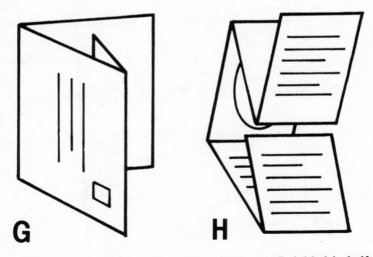

G. *The Classic:* A simple 6″ x 9″ or 8½″ x 11″, folded in half. Easy to read, inexpensive to print. Understood by the reader.

H. *The Shuffle:* This mailer is meant to entertain and hopefully not confuse. There are many ways you can open this piece so each message must be able to stand alone.

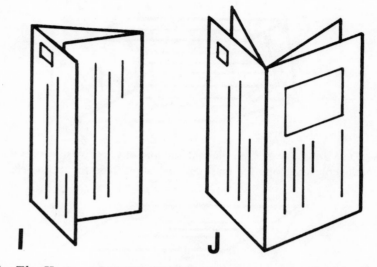

I. *The Horizontal/Single Flip:* Good style to have the customer open and read an important message on the facing page that explains what they are about to see on the double page coming up.

J. *The Double Classic:* Same as G. Just another section added.

K. *The Triple Split Definitive:* The same as "C." Only three times as much.

L. *The Vertical Single Flip:* The same as "I." Only turned around.

M. *The Double Peak:* A little clumsy in handling but opens to a big finish. Good if you want to show a giant photograph.

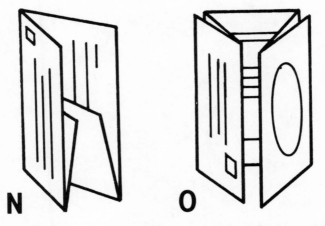

N. *The Presentation Fold.* Just like a brochure from a company. Only much simpler. Can use to tuck in ads in the folds. Many department stores do this as a mini-catalog.

O. *Double Gate.* Like the name says. There are two ways to get into this message.

P. *The Claccord.* Our contraction of the Classic Fold combined with the Accordian Fold.

Q. *Over & Under.* Good style to use for a die-cut to tease the reader into what's waiting for him if he keeps on reading.

These are just a few of the many variations of folds you can make. Combining one with another (like the Claccord) gives you an even greater variety.

Important: Check with your printer so he can tell you what his folding machine can (and cannot) do. The machine only folds in certain mysterious ways. Work with what is available.

9
What Type Are You?

WE RUN AN AD in the newspaper every day, always in the same position.

The typeface is always the same. Typefaces have names like you and me. Sometimes it's the name of the person who designed the type face: Benguiat, Lubalin, Goudy. Sometimes it simply matches what the typeface looks like.

Computer looks like computer type. *American Typewriter* looks like typewriter printing.

The typeface we use in our newspaper ad is called *Tiffany Medium.* A sophisticated, easily recognizable look.

One day we ran our regular store ad using the Tiffany Medium typeface. We were advertising boy's jackets on sale.

Good ad. Except the newspaper left off the name of our store!

We called up our ad rep and complained. He apologized and said they would run the ad again at the end of the week, with our name, at no charge.

Fine. But it wouldn't help us sell the sale jackets *that* day.

Except we sold thirty-five *that day!*

We waited on the last customer ourselves. She asked to see the jackets on sale. We showed them and she bought one. Before she left we asked how she knew about the sale. "I saw your ad in the paper today," she said.

We quickly grabbed a copy of the ad and showed it to her, "But it doesn't have our name in the ad!" we said.

She examined it very carefully then looked up and said, "In *my* paper at home . . . it has your name."

What was she saying?

This: She knew it was our ad because it "looked like" our ad. *Because the typeface we use gave our business a simple and recognizable identity.*

Since type is better shown than explained, we have some illustrations on the following pages as well as in the TOOLBOX at the end of this chapter. But for now, let's list Ten Commandments for selecting type for your direct mailer:

COMMANDMENT I. First, remember type has a first impression. The book *Dress for Success* by John T. Malloy says there's a strong relationship between how you look and how you succeed.

Your business "look" extends beyond the façade of the building and the design of the interior. There is an instant identification the customer makes when he first sees your mailer. What your mailer looks like is what forms that impression. And what "type" you are is determined by what typeface you use.

That's one advantage type has for you: *type helps create your identification.*

Do not let the printer set your ads and direct mail in any type he wants. *You* pick and choose what *you* want and tell him. Otherwise your ad becomes everyone's ad or worse, somebody else's instead.

Just as your name of your business is easily recognized by your logo or symbols, so is your advertiseing. The eye is a creature of habit. It remembers what it has seen before.

You take your three-year-old child out for a ride in the car. She points to a billboard and says, "Look, Coca-Cola!" Can she read at three years old? No. What she saw was a "picture" conveyed by the way the Coca-Cola script appears.

The child "knew" what it was . . . because of the type. Reason why: The eye recognizes *shapes* more than letters. (See serif *vs* sans serif in the TOOLBOX section).

COMMANDMENT II. Type has personality. Some are fat. Some are skinny. Some are tall. Some are short. Some are masculine. Some are feminine. Some are plain and some are fancy.

Choose a typeface that you think "looks like" your business. Show different typefaces to friends, customers. "Which one do you think looks like my business?" You'll be surprised how many will choose the same one. (We have included some commonly used styles in the TOOLBOX at the end of this chapter.)

COMMANDMENT III. Type has sound. It translates how you want to talk to your readers. The big bold headline is a shout. The small type is a lot of white space and a whisper. Type can have an upper class accent or be contemporary slang.

COMMANDMENT IV. Type creates a mood. The local discount store has one typeface look, the department store still another and the sophisticated specialty shop yet another. Each typeface would not work if used in place of another.

That is one of the tests. Does the typeface look as though it belongs to *your* business. Does it have the "feel" and the "look" of who you are. Remember, you must have a look before you have an image.

COMMANDMENT V. Type must be readable. There is a typeface called Times Roman still used by the London Times newspaper. Today it used by more than 70 percent of the newspapers in the English-speaking world. The reason: *it is easy to read.** Next point: Make type big enough to read. There are now more senior citizens in the U.S. than teenagers.

COMMANDMENT VI. Type should be background music. Every movie you see has music. The purpose is to heighten your interest and hint at future developments. But the most effective background music is *not* noticeable. It creates an atmosphere but is not recognizable by itself. And so it is with good typefaces. They help to create the mood and interest but do not call attention to themselves.

COMMANDMENT VII. Type faces should rarely be used in reverse. That means white type on a black background. The reason not to use this style is that it violates Commandment V.

COMMANDMENT VIII. Type should be a close-knit family. Keep out the *relatives*. Many direct mail pieces use a half a dozen or more different typefaces. This makes the message confusing and difficult to read and follow (and buy from).

COMMANDMENT IX. Type should have breathing room. Leave enough white space between words and especially between lines. Make it easier for the eye to read your message. Look how much moredifficultit istoreadthis. Is there a rule for the proper space? Sure. Whatever looks good to you. Experiment and see what a big difference a little space can make.

COMMANDMENT X. Type must stand alone to be individual. Do not set type on top of a tint or texture or a color. It will not stand out clearly. It will not be read. And the merchandise will not be bought.

Most important of all: Type is simply communication. It is the translation of *how* you want to talk to your readers.

---

*Which is why we used it for this book.

TOOLBOX

In the little more than 500 years since Gutenberg printed his Bible in the mid-1400s, nearly 10,000 different typefaces have appeared, each with its own name. The one you are reading right now is called Times Roman.

Originally, italic typefaces resembled the handwriting they replaced. Roman faces were based on inscriptions chiseled in stone. Soon designers began to construct their own type styles, using their own names for identity.

In 1734, a graphic artist in England named William Caslon, designed his first type. The style was so popular it was introduced in the American colonies by Benjamin Franklin and chosen by a Baltimore printer for the first official copies of the Declaration of Independence.

Today there are hundreds of type faces. And each a name and a personality. And each with a complete family. (That means they usually come regular and bold and light *face*. Which is how thick or heavy they appear on paper.)

Typefaces not only have different names but also come in different sizes. In type language, there are 72 "points" to an inch.

Most type comes in sizes from 6 to 72 points. Some type goes up to 120 points (see headlines on tabloid newspapers.) The larger the number, the bigger the type. What you are reading right now is 10 point. The size of the type in the classified ads in your local paper is probably 6 point.

When typesetters talk about type, they have their own language and definitions. When we talk about how wide something is we think of inches and feet (if its *real* wide). The printer talks about picas. One pica is 12 points. Translation: A line of type 4 inches wide is 24 picas.

This is 6 point type.

This is 18 point type.

Type larger than 14 point is usually display type, used for headings and base lines. Body copy is set in smaller sizes. Most type comes in light, medium, or bold face (the weight of the type).

Is there a right type size for your mailer? Not really. Just big enough to read. (At least 8 point, 10 point is better.) Newspaper layouts are often as follows: The headlines are at least 24 point, the body type is 8 to 10 points. There *is* a relationship between the size of the type and the length of the line. Guide: 35 to 40 characters to a line (each space and letter is a character) is easy to read.

Serif *vs* Sans-serif

Serifs are the little "hooks" you see on the edges of letters. This book is set in serif type because the little "hooks" or strokes on the bottom of the letters give the letters "shape" and make them easier to read.

Many of the newer typefaces are sans serif, as explained and set in the next paragraph.

More modern type faces are referred to as sans serif (without the strokes). This is fine if the type is set big enough like this. But difficult to read if printed too tiny like this.

Final Note: Type manufacturers publish books on typefaces. Newspapers have their own type books. So do printers. Call your newspaper and printer now. Ask each of them to send you a book of the different typefaces they carrry so you can decide what "type" you are or want to be in future mailers. And you can have a *free* subscription to a fascinating newspaper on typography called *U&lc* (for *U*pper and *L*ower *C*ase). That means capital letters and letters that are not capitalized.

Write them for your free subscription. Here's the address:

U & lc
2 Dag Hammarskjold Plaza
New York, New York 10017

The reason this ad "looks" Colonial is . . . The typefaces used in colonial times were made of wood, not metal. The constant slamming of the metal printing plate against the wooden typefaces made edges break off. That's why much colonial printing has this "broken edge" look. The name of the typeface created to achieve the same effect is Caslon Antique. A good example of how a typeface conveys a time and an effect.

Would you buy **women's designer jeans** that sell for $40 to $48 on sale at **19.99.** THEN CALL TÉRI AT 344-5000 IN OUR WOMEN'S SHOP. SHE'LL TELL YOU ABOUT OUR DENIM AND TWILL JEANS RIGHT FROM REG. STOCK BY KATHY HARDWICKE, COMPLI-MENTS AND JONES SPORT WE SELL TO $40-$48 ON SALE FOR $19.99. SIZES 4-14. IN THE WOMEN'S SHOP IN GORDON'S IN....

Gordon's Alley atlantic city, n.j. 344-5000 free parking on s. penna. avenue next to firehouse

Quick! What Does the Headline Say? If your eye quickly scans this headline you will see only four words: "Women's designer jeans $19.99." Reason why: the type is set *bold face* because the most important words stand out that way.

Use bold face in your type to emphasize certain points and/or to provide a break in a long column of regular type.

FREE monogramming on men's, women's and children's pullover sweaters. **FREE** hand painted names on jog suits. **FREE** Ralph Lauren make-up consultation. **FREE** names on Alley bags. **FREE** mini book lamps*. And more when you shop the shops in Gordon's Alley today through Labor Day.

Open today, Friday and Saturday: 9:30 to 6:00
Open Sunday and Labor Day Monday: 10 to 2

The most powerful word in the English language is "FREE," so let's use it a lot. The ad begins with "Free" and the word is repeated four more times throughout the headline. Notice it is also set in bold face type so that a quick glance at the headline merely shows a lot of "free" some-things . . . Hmmmm, better go back and read it more carefully to see what they are.

THIS AD IS IN LARGE TYPE BECAUSE WE WANT TO CALL YOUR ATTENTION TO THE BIGGEST COLUMBUS DAY SALE IN OUR 38-YEAR HISTORY: MONDAY, OCTOBER 8, 1984. WE OPEN AT 9 A.M.

I'M SHOUTING SO YOU CAN HEAR ME!! This ad ran in the newspaper, and the size of the headline you see above was four times the size of this page. (We shrunk it down to fit.)

What it does: It yells. It screams. It calls attention to. The letters are all in capital letters and the ad loudly announces: "Look at me. I'm important!"

A good headline to run in a mailer but only once in a while. Otherwise it's like the street noises when you visit the city. The first night you can't sleep because of the noise. But soon the sound blends into the background and you no longer hear the clamor.

Not just another pretty face . . .

Easiest read type face English Times	**Classy / elegant** Tiffany Medium	**Old Fashioned** Bodoni Bold
Feminine Florentine Script	*Sophisticated* Park Avenue	**A Christmas Carol** Old English
Most popular type face Helios Light	**Masculine** Goudy heavyface	**Computer look** Geometric Bold
Looks like it's typed American Typewriter	Light, delicate Avant Garde extra light	ART DECO LOOK Busorama Medium

Every typeface has a meaning all its own . . . Underneath each of the typefaces we have listed the *name* of that particular typeface. Then we have set, in that type face, a description.

EXAMPLE: The typeface "Old English" has a *Christmas Carol* "look." The typeface "American Typewriter" looks like it has been typed.

When you're trying to sell a specific product or time of the year, look at the typefaces available to see which tells that story best.

10
Show Your Colors!

W E ONCE HAD an insurance agent who loved the color orange. He used the color orange in his advertising. The morning mail would always have a stack of white envelopes. If there was an orange envelope, we would say, "I wonder what my insurance agent is writing me about today?"

He wore orange ties. And carried a pocketful of little pieces of orange candy he would hand you on the street, at a meeting, at a luncheon or dinner. The local children's hospital regularly received a crate of oranges from him.

And then the day came when a young woman opened up a dress shop of her own in our town and painted the front door orange. And the citizens of the town would walk by and say, "How about that . . . an insurance agent opening a dress shop . . ."

That's what color does.

It identifies you. Your store. Your product. Your merchandise.

Once you decide on a color for your business use it all the time. The colors for our store are beige and brown. (It's also the colors for Saks 5th Avenue and if you mix us up with them . . . that's O.K.)

Quick now: What's the name of the chocolate candy with the chocolate and white letters?

What's the name of the soup in the red and white can?

What mouthwash is green?

What toothpaste is multicolored?

See how it works? You associate a color with a product and/or vice versa.

And so, folks, what color is *your business?* Is there a specific color which, when seen, brings the name of your business to mind? There should be. And when you do your direct mail pieces you can incorporate your colors into your mailing piece.

135

Pay attention to color. It *will* affect your mailings. It *will* make a difference in whether or not your mail is read, paid attention to and (most important) acted upon.

What do colors do? They soothe. They excite. They activate emotions.

And since emotions are only a half-step away from buying (or *not* buying), let us review colors and what they do and don't do.

Men seem to respond best to earth tones: the nature colors, the browns, rusts, grays, greens, blues.

Women seem to respond best to softer colors. Pastels, pure white, shiny black.

Blues and greens are genderless. They seem to appeal to either sex.

Colors also convey a meaning. Red can mean embarrassment (blush), a country (China), evasion (herring), delay (tape), or stop (light). White can mean Broadway (Great White Way), purity or the hats the Dodge boys used to wear.

Blue can mean a nursery rhyme (Little Boy), a painting (boy), a killer (beard), or sadness. Pink can be a state of health or a sign you are out of work. Green can be envy, inexperience, a sign to go or the pastures to lie down in. Yellow is a taxi, a coward, a sign of caution, or a ribbon tied around an old oak tree.

Gold is silence, not all the glitters, the fleece sought by Jason or the rule to guide your life. (To which our local financial expert said the Golden Rule for bankers is simply: "Those that have the gold, rule.")

Gray does seem to connote conservatism and age from the flannel suit of the same color to Geoffrey Beene's cologne of the same name or the time your mirror suggests a change to Grecian Formula.

Sometimes colors become positively chameleon from the well-known horse (the one of a different color) to the panther that was a black civil rightist, a pink detective, and a grey senior citizen.

Colors can also be one word descriptions: rust (wears out); lemon (bad wares); raspberry (wherever you're criticized).

Artist Eloise Barnhurt says, "Red is the color of sex and yellow is a nerve energizer that keeps us awake." And it is true that blue connotes truth, wisdom and loyalty.

Here are some facts about color:

Fact: You *can* increase mailing results with a wise choice of colored paper and/or colored ink.

Fact: Colored stationery and envelopes outpull white stationery and envelopes.

Fact: For every test that tells you one color pulls better than another, there is another test that tells you the reverse is also true.

Fact: When everyone who reads this book convinces everyone else to use color in the mailings, the one remaining person using black and white will probably achieve the best results. Because his envelope will be the only white one in that mail.

Fact: Red and purple mean "action." Good colors for sales.

Fact: Adding a second color will increase sales.

Fact: Adding a third and fourth color will not necessarily increase sales. (*Exception:* Food. Clothing. Furniture. And then, only if the color reproduction is excellent.)

Fact: Your personal color favorite is probably the wrong one to use for a second color. What color best reflects the job, the store, the reason for using?

Fact: Less is more. Famous architect Mies van der Rohe had it right when he said the less you use, the more dramatic the results. Picture a page chock full of red color. Picture the same page in black and white with a single dot of red color. Which page attracts your interest more?

Fact: Order or reply forms printed in colored ink and/or colored stock will outpull order forms printed in black ink on white stock.

Fact: There is some test, somewhere by somebody that will prove to you all the above facts do not work.

But since you've got to start *somewhere,* try these. They *do* work. (Well, . . . most of the time.)

What all this means: If colors set off predictable emotional reactions (they do), why not adapt and adopt the positive reactions for your store or business (you should).

When you reassociate your business with an established positive color, you have taken a giant step toward bringing your customer to read what you write and buy what you sell.

Any doubts you may have as to the success of this philosophy will disappear after the next rainfall. Simply look into the sky and see the rainbow (which is all colors) and you will remember what awaits you at its end.

TOOLBOX

Specifying Color

Most printers not specializing in color normally have their presses running black ink. A different (standard) ink color is usually no more expensive, but you might have to pay a small charge for a press "cleanup" to change to your color.

Most color specifying for printing is based on the commercial system devised by Pantone, Inc., and the system is referred to as the PANTONE®* MATCHING SYSTEM. There are eight PANTONE Basic Colors plus PANTONE Black and PANTONE Transparent White, from which all PANTONE Colors are made. The formulation of colors depends on the percentages of each of these PANTONE Basic Colors used.

To standardize color specifying, Pantone publishes a variety of color guides and reference books, each with hundreds of possible color combinations shown on coated and uncoated paper, along with PANTONE MATCHING SYSTEM identifying numbers.

Each additional color of ink adds to your printing bill—but there are ways to give the effect of different colors without actually changing the basic ink used. You can use papers of various colors to create a two-color look. Some colors, however, do not overprint on the colors satisfactorily.

Screens or tints of the colors selected produce lighter versions of the ink used (again, shown in color specifying references) and give you a two color effect without two-color cost.

If you are printing both sides of your paper, you can have stock with one color on one side and white on the other.

When planning a mailing piece, consider how it will be folded. With some folds, color on one side will show up, when folded, as color on two sides.

Four color (full color) printing is expensive but often necessary in direct mail packages, particularly for the brochure or selling piece accompanying the letter. This usually is not an in-house or do-it-yourself function,

*Pantone, Inc.'s check-standard trademark for color reproduction and color reproduction materials.
Pantone, Inc., 55 Knickerbocker Road, Moonachie, NJ 07074

and printers with the right equipment and experience to do a satisfactory job. The do-it-yourself concept simply requires a basic understanding of the color printing process.

Cutting Color Costs

Here are a few suggestions that will often make color more afffordable than you would think.

Plan your printing time to coincide with jobs your printer may be running using the same color you want, or, find out what colors he may be running that would be satisfactory for your job.

Exact color matches add to cost. You may find a standard color that is satisfactory.

Specifying large areas of color coverage on a sheet adds to your cost.

Bleeds—carrying color to the very edges of the printed sheet—adds to the cost.

Some printers, particularly postcard printers, gang-run full-color pieces, usually on both postcard stock and on coated stock. By having your piece done with others, you can greatly reduce the price of full color.

Although some artists may not fully understand the use of color in selling, they can be very helpful in getting your concept onto paper in a form that can be properly handled by the printer. Graphic designers (their fees will be higher) can give you more detailed help with color selection.

Work closely with your printer and well in advance of your needed date. Chances are your printer can offer additional suggestions that will save both time and money.

11
What's So Special About Specialties?

THERE IS A SCENE in the musical *Gypsy* where the young Gypsy Rose Lee is instructed by some of the older and more experienced burlesque professionals. "If you wanna be successful," they say, "ya gotta have a gimmick."

Gimmicks are what makes your mailer stand out—apart from and (we hope) in front of the competition. One way you can do this is with direct mail's best kept secret: the advertising specialty.

At the many seminars in which we participate, we often ask the question, "How many of you know what an advertising specialty is?"

"Do you mean most people think we are advertising specialists?"

No, folks, what we mean *are* "specialties."

Correctly defined, advertising specialties are inexpensive, useful items imprinted with an advertiser's name, logo or message, which are given out freely—no strings attached.*

Pens, pencils, key chains and calendars are a few of those things that often come to mind. Beyond these specialties there are thousands of other items that can be used with or without imprinting to substantially improve your direct mail results. Not unlike direct mail, specialties have suffered under the "junk" stigma. They have been called gimmicks, novelties, trinkets and, worse yet, "throwaways." We'll agree that they are often novel. We'll agree that in a sense they are a gimmick. We will not, however, agree to the "throwaway" designation.

Just as we ask the question at seminars, "Do you know what a specialty is?" we also ask if the people in the audience have any specialties on their person. Almost everyone has some imprinted advertising specialty on or with them—many received in the mail.

*Items given away with a real or implied obligation on the part of the recipient are known as premiums. (See TOOL BOX at the end of chapter.)

141

Let's look at some of the things found among both men and women in a typical audience. There are the most common items—the pencils, pens, key chains and wallet calendars we talked about earlier—and more: a wallet-size airport directory listing all of the phone numbers for the airlines, car rental agencies and hotels in the major city served by a charter air service; a comb, enclosed in a greeting card from a local barber shop; a cowboy-style belt buckle emblazoned with the word *Dallas* mailed by a trade association to attract attendees to a convention in . . . guess where?

And there were billfolds, wallets and money clips that had been mailed. Industrial companies mailed eyeglass lens cleaners, rulers and scales, pocket flashlights and screw drivers. Beauty parlors sent emery boards and nail files; retail stores were represented with sample vials of perfume. A hotel included a pack of plastic toothpicks in a mailing whose headline read, "Now you can have the pick of meeting sites."

Advertising specialties are not "throwaways." The industry has been referred to as "remembrance advertising" or the "thank you" medium . . . and we agree. Forget the cost; it's the thought that counts.

Not unlike direct mail, specialty advertising has some distinct marketing advantages over the more popular media, including message retention, versatility and low cost. It also shares with direct mail the advantage of being a targeted and personal medium. And uniquely, specialty advertising is really a fun medium. People enjoy receiving a gift, however small, and you can "Put a little fun in your life when you put a little life in your promotions."

Now let's combine the advantages of the two media—direct mail and specialty advertising—to reap the rewards of increased returns and results.

To your typical package (the envelope with teaser copy, the letter, the brochure and the business reply vehicle) add an advertising specialty. It can be as simple as the wallet calendar or as complex as a series of items mailed throughout the year. The cost can range from a few pennies to several dollars.

Studies show that recipients believe companies that have their names on unique or substantial items are unique or substantial companies.

How does the specialty help the mailing?

1. The specialty can help get the envelope or package opened—particularly if the specialty has bulk or relates to the teaser copy on the envelope. The imprinted message or logo on the specialty item serves as a reminder of the mailer or offer long after the rest of the package has been discarded.

2. The specialty can tie together the theme, the sender's name or product.

3. The specialty may be used as an element of surprise or as an attention-getter.

4. The specialty acts as a "thank you" for past business in the same mailing that solicits new business. (Remember, your *best* prospects are your *current* customers.)

The Opportunities to use specialties to enhance direct mail results seem almost limitless (see TOOLBOX for 100 Ways to Use Specialties).

Here are a few case histories of direct mail campaigns used by a variety of businesses, professionals and charities which produced unusual results.

Not-for-Profit Group

The local women's chapter of the Gettysburg College (Pennsylvania) alumni association traditionally mails their fund solicitation letters in early December. With contributions lagging, they switched to a February mailing to arrive on or just before Valentine's Day—and for the first time, included specialties.

The first year, a heart-shaped key tag accompanied the letter and business reply envelope, the copy on the key tag, "I Have a Love Affair With Gettysburg." Contributions increased 15 to 20 percent.

The next year, a heart-shaped cloth appliqué was attached to the letter and the alumnus was encouraged to wear the heart on Valentines Day. Contributions were up 25 percent over the *previous* year.

Next year: the "I Love Gettysburg" labels used by parents or students on envelopes and stationery. Results: greater increases over the previous year.

The most recent: a thin heart-shaped magnet attached to the letter by means of a special metal patch affixed to the letter with adhesive. The copy read, "Thanks for Opening Your Heart for Gettysburg." The magnet could be used to hang messages on refrigerators, desks, file cabinets and just about anywhere suitable metal was available.

Now the campaign had exposure all year long!

Manufacturer

Judy/Instructo is a Minneapolis-based manufacturer of children's educational toys. Every year there is a convention of the country's leading wholesalers of this product and Judy/Instructo takes a booth to show their wares.

Last year (1985) they had a large range of new toys. They were proud of their new, expanded line. Now, how could they attract the buyers to their booth?

They mailed each wholesaler a package a month before the show. Their theme: "We're tooting our own horn." They said they were so proud of their new items they wanted to announce the fact to everyone and included a toy kazoo in the package. They invited the customer to come to their booth, play the kazoo and win a free prize!

There were 335 wholesalers that attended the trade fair and *every one* came to the Judy/Instructo booth. Some had practiced for weeks on special songs on the kazoo, played their number and received a prize.

A specialty sales item returned a 100 percent attendance and resulted in nearly a 75% increase in sales over the previous year's show.

Industrial Distributor

A distributor of fasteners took on a new line of threaded nuts. He wanted to introduce the line quickly to his customers. At the same time he also wanted to let his customers and prospects know that he was providing a toll-free 800 number for their convenience.

His first thought was a newsletter approach, but he was willing to consider an advertising specialty.

We suggested a key ring with a portion made of plastic to resemble a round telephone dial. The number appearing in the center of the dial? His new toll-free number.

Next: A sample of one of the nuts from the new line was slipped onto the key ring and the ring reassembled. The key ring was mailed in a cloth bag with envelope attached—typical of envelopes used to mail industrial samples. The envelope contained a letter explaining the new line and listing the new telephone number with a business reply card for requesting catalogs, prices and further samples.

Additionally, a self-adhesive label showing the new number (which could be attached to a phone) was also enclosed.

Response?

"Our phones were humming with requests for catalog and pricing information just days after the first pieces went into the mail," the distributor commented. "It was probably the fastest reaction we've ever had to a new line."

Churches

A church serving a middle-class suburban neighborhood wanted to reach the families in a three-mile radius to make known their various community outreach programs. The available weekly newspaper's much wider circulation posed the problem of overkill—more response than could be handled. Direct mail seemed the answer to reach a target market inexpensively. There was, however, a second problem. People might not need, or realize they need, help when they received the mailing. How could you get them to remember the services for an extended period of time?

A bent pencil imprinted with the church's hotline number and this message was enclosed:

> Your life need straightening out?
> For help with marital, financial,
> alcohol or drug problems
> CALL US!

Results: The program was quickly fully subscribed.

Professionals

It wasn't too long ago when professionals couldn't advertise. Now that they can, many—if not most—still suffer pangs about seeing their names in print, or worse yet, having their colleagues see their names in print.

Perhaps professionals, more than most business people, recognize that their clients (customers) are their best source of new business.

They rely on referrals. To get their clients or patients to remember them between visits and to encourage word-of-mouth referrals, many professionals have turned to direct mail . . . and specialty advertising.

New IRS rules provide both lawyers and accountants with the opportunity to mail not only the information explaining the new rules but also the means for keeping the necessary records. A wide variety of forms, booklets and diaries—all imprinted with professionals' names and addresses—were mailed to clients. When used, they provide daily ad message exposure for an entire year.

Specialties specialize in not only calling attention to a specific mailing but serve as a reminder for weeks and months after the original letter has been forgotten.

TOOLBOX

To better understand the Specialty Advertising Industry, a basic knowledge of terminology is essential since so many people tend to confuse advertising specialties with premiums, gifts and prizes.

- Advertising Specialty—a useful, usually inexpensive item imprinted with a name, logo or sales message which is given away freely, no strings attached.
- Premium—an item, sometimes imprinted, but mostly not, given as an inducement to make a purchase or to take some other action as part of a promotion program. It has strings attached—you must do something to gain the premium. Premiums can vary in price from under $1.00 to hundreds or even thousands of dollars.
- Gifts—given by suppliers of products or services to customers or prospects. They are hardly ever imprinted and vary in price, starting at about $5.00 and going as high as one wants to go. (Current income tax regulations permit deductions for business gifts only up to $25.00).
- Prizes—used in connection with contests. They are usually not imprinted and can vary in costs, but recipient may be subject to federal income tax for the value of the prize.

Buying Specialties, Premiums, Gifts and Prizes

Part of the confusion in terminology arises from the way the above items are sold, with overlap among all categories.

Advertising Specialties—sold through a network of independent advertising specialty distributors, referred to in the industry as Counselors. These organizations can vary in size and competence from single person operations selling pens, pencils, key chains, etc., from catalogs and a sample case to fully staffed agencies prepared to furnish creative concepts, art, photography, copy, warehousing, and even distribution to the recipients.

Additionally, there are suppliers known as Direct Houses that both manufacture and sell their own products and sometimes products of other industry suppliers. Specialties are also sold through catalogs, on a selected item basis, by direct mail sources (who do not offer any services beyond imprinting). In addition to selling advertising specialties, counselors may also sell premiums, prizes, gifts, incentives and awards with these items frequently being specialties without imprints.

Premiums—primarily sold by premium representatives, individual agents representing a number of premium lines.

Business Gifts—sold by both premium representatives and advertising specialty counselors, but are also available from executive shopping services, or can be purchased directly from retail stores.

Prizes—again, available from premium representatives and advertising specialty counselors.

Incentives—The same items that serve as premiums or gifts can also be used in incentive programs to stimulate marketing action and they too are available from specialty advertising counselors and/or permium representatives.

Awards and Recognition—Plaques, jewelry, clocks, silverware etc., usually engraved or imprinted with a congratulatory message, are also available from specialty advertising counselors and premium representatives.

For the purposes of direct mail, advertising specialties can probably take care of all your needs. Refer to the "Advertising Specialties" section in the Yellow Pages of your local phone directory.

What to Expect of an Specialty Advertising Counselor

When you take the first step and decide to use advertising specialties, you've already made a commitment to creativity in your mailing. The Counselor, above all, should have the ability to augment your creative efforts. The Counselor should be an "idea" person and have the facilities and willingness to provide research and samples to help you find the specialty or premium that fits your package.

Assured availability and on-time delivery of the selected specialty are the responsibility of the Counselor. Because of imprinting or personalization, expect an average delivery time of four to six weeks . . . and expect your Counselor to follow up, keep you posted and make sure you get on-time delivery. Don't let the specialty be the cause of a late mailing.

What Not to Expect From an Specialty Advertising Counselor

Advertising specialties tend to be reasonably priced with mark-ups designed to adequately compensate the Counselor for providing all the services you require. Although some Counselors may offer discounted prices, you must remember that discounts often reflect the services provided. Volume discounts are available as part of industry pricing practices and, depending on the circumstances, Counselors may absorb art and shipping charges (most specialties are shipped FOB factory, with the purchaser paying the freight).

The Counselor who does the research and provides a creative solution to your problem deserves the order. If *you* come up with the product through your own research, "shopping" is an acceptable business practice.

The best approach, however, is to find a competent Counselor or representative for premiums and establish a working relationship for your continuing needs. Under some circumstances the factories, through the Counselor, may offer free speculative samples ("spec" samples from your artwork). Don't, however, expect a Counselor to provide liberal or expensive samples—they normally are billed.

Publications

A variety of publications serve the Specialty and Premium industries, including:

Imprint—a quarterly publication offered free by many Counselors to customers and good prospects. It contains case histories of successful campaigns utilizing specialties along with product advertisements.

Counselor—the monthly trade publication restricted to Counselors and their suppliers. It is used as a source for news of the industry, new products, case histories, how-to articles, etc.

Potentials in marketing—a monthly tabloid with news about advertising specialties, premiums, gifts for the marketing executive. (A Lakeland Publication, 50 South Ninth Street, Minneapolis, MN 55402; Phone: (612) 333-0471.)

Premium Incentive Business—a monthly tabloid devoted to the premium and incentive industry. An annual directory is published each year in February listing suppliers and products. Available from: Gralla Publications, 1515 Broadway, New York, NY 10036.

Incentive Marketing—An incentive-oriented monthly magazine which also includes information on travel incentives. Published by: Hartman Communications, Inc., 633 Third Ave., New York, NY 10017.

The only up-to-date book available on Specialty Advertising is *Specialty Advertising: New Dimensions in Creative Marketing,* by George L. L. Herpel and Steve Slack. Specialty Advertising Association International, Irving, Texas. 75062.

Trade Information Sources

The Advertising Specialty Institute provides a variety of services exclusively to bona fide specialty advertising counselors and distributors, including a uniform alpha-numeric identification system used for filing, product information retrieval, records, reference and data processing.

Trade Associations

The trade association for the specialty advertising business is:
Specialty Advertising Association International
P.O. Box 85247
Dallas, TX 75285

101 Inexpensive Imprinted Advertising Specialty Items

Address Books	Holiday Decorations	Pins
Adhesive Strips	Ice Scrapers	Playing Cards
Appliques	Insurance Wallets	Pocket Protectors
Ash Trays	Jar Openers	Poker Chips
Atlas (miniature)	Jewelry	Posters
Badges	Key Chains	Pot Holders
Balloons	Knives	Pot Scrapers
Book Covers	Labels	Puppets, Hand
Booklets	Lens Cleaners	Puzzles
Bookmarks	Letter Openers	Rainhats
Bumper Stickers	Lint Removers	Recipe Books
Business Card Cases	Litter Bags	Rulers
Buttons	Lucky Charms	Screwdrivers
Calculators (paper)	Luggage Tags	Seeds
Calendars	Magic Tricks	Sewing Kits
Candy	Magnets	Shoe Horns
Charts—Slide	Magnifiers	Shoe Laces
Coin Purses	Manicure Tools	Signs
Coins	Maps	Simulated Money
Combs	Membership Cards	Slide Rules
Cookbooks	Message Holders	Soap
Coupon Cutters	Miniature Tools	Spatulas
Coupon Holders	Mirrors	Sponges
Currency Converters	Models—Planes	Sports Schedules
Diaries	Money Clips	Stamp Holders
Fans	Nailfiles	Stamps
Fishing Lures	Notebooks	Tablets
First Aid Guides	Paperclips	Tape Measures
Flags	Patches	Telephone Directories
Flowers (artificial)	Pencils	Tie Clips
Fly Swatters	Pens	Tie Tacks
Games	Phone Aids	Thermometers
Gift Certificates	Photo Holders	Tooth Picks
Golf Tees	Photos	

101 Situations Where Imprinted Advertising Specialities Can Be Used*

Supplement other advertising efforts
Establish prestige
Reduce prejudices
Create corporate indentity
Build broadcast audience
Spotlight favorable publicity
Make customer feel important
Obtain third party endorsements
Imply third party endorsements
Introduce new service
Introduce new management
Serve as souvenir in gift shop
Build customer loyalty
Round out marketing plan
Serve as dealer loader
Symbolize friendship
Promote meeting attendance
Collect from delinquent accounts
Reduce entertainment costs
Reward sales force
Raise funds
Commemorate special occasions
Encourage quality control
Symbolize safety effort to OSHA
Stimulate window displays
Symbolize new promotional campaign
Announce marketing plans
Symbolically apologize
Discourage brand substitution
Deliver institutional message
Tell success story
Publicize company policy
Increase catalog distribution
Stimulate work-of-mouth advertising

Serve as sample holder
Produce direct sales
Educate prospects about needs
Promote early buying
Enhance direct mail response
Target message to influentials
Create new buying habits
Stimulate grand opening traffic
Reduce required sales calls
Enhance employee pride in company
Impress present stockholders
Stimulate information requests
Enhance product distinctiveness
Improve community relations
Keep company's name in buyer's mind
Encourage trial usage
Reach altogether new target groups
Strengthen brand loyalty
Give sales reps something new to discuss
Increase psychological involvement
Enlist spouse's support
Extend peak sales season
Focus appeal to a specific segment
Produce sales leads
Stimulate sample ordering
Help organize sales presentations
Get users to recommend company
Increase product usage
Spotlight product or service features
Attract new users
Reach hard-to-see prospects
Test pulling power on an ad medium
Appeal to competitor's customers
Promote multiple-unit sales

Improve employee loyalty
Attract new stockholders
Discourage competing salespeople
Boost p-o-p sales
Welcome to community
Reduce vandalism
Promote demonstrations
Encourage use of p-o-p
Project ideas for new users
Offset competitive promotions
Offset seasonal slump
Give recognition for achievement
Encourage opening charge accounts
Reduce employee turnover
Announce new phone or address
Celebrate anniversary
Recruitment
Promoting branch openings
Introducing new products/services
Motivating salesmen/sales department employees
Opening new accounts
Stimulating sales meetings
Developing trade show traffic
Balancing improper product mix
Activating inactive accounts
Changing names or products
Using sales aids for door openers
Motivating consumers through premiums
Moving products at dealer level
Improving client or customer relations
Building an image
Motivating employees
Promoting new facilities
Introducing new salesmen

*Dr. Dan F. Bagley III, Ph.D. University of South Florida, USA.

12
The Envelope Please

Q UESTION: When your customers receive their morning mail, which envelope do they open first?

ANSWER: The one that captures their attention. The pile of white envelopes is nothing more than a pile of white envelopes. If one is an odd color, you pause, look again. If one is mailed from a foreign country, you pause, look again. If one is a different shape, you pause, look again. If one has a strong message on the outside offering a personal benefit you pause . . . and look again.

We call this the Pause that Catches.

In a split second or two, your customers must be convinced your letter is more important than all the other letters they received in the morning mail.

It all begins with the envelope.

And if you ask, "What about the secretary who *first* sees the mail," the answer is simply the same: How do you have the secretary pause and catch her attention?

People who send out direct mail know this works, and there is a continuing game of can-you-top-this in clever, different and unusual envelope designs. These are done through a difference in shape, size, style, color or texture of paper.

The trap here is you can become so clever in doing something different that everyone simply says, "My isn't that clever". . . and moves on to the next white envelope with a message *they* want to read.

So the opening rule for the envelope opening is it is not enough to be simply clever. You must also have something to say *that the reader wants to read.*

This "something to say" can be actual words or a "look" that makes someone react immediately as they would if a telephone rang in their office.

How do we have the envelope be a ringing telephone?

Obvious ways: a Federal Express package. Or a Telegram. These are all loud alarms that make the reader pay attention. They are effective. But expensive.

What are some of the ideas about envelopes that seem to work most of the time?

In this chapter we will give you ideas about envelopes, how to make them interesting and eye appealing and how to create a desire to be opened by the consumer/customer/prospect.

Bill Jayme puts together one successful mailing package after another with his designer partner, Heikki Ratalahti. Here's what he says about envelopes.

"We spend about one-third of our time putting together the outer envelope. Sometimes we will use an eye-catching graphic. Or a single word written large. ("Damn!" read a bold display for a business magazine!) The word "free" often appears in a window cut-out to have the reader open the envelope.

"The envelope is the display window in the department store," says Jayme, "the sleeve on the record album, the hot pants on a hooker." Jayme suggests you ask yourself three key questions when you finish putting together the envelope for your direct mailer.

1. Does your outer envelope ring the doorbell loud and clear or just timidly knock?

2. Does your package look and sound like your product? Or like every other product?

3. When the prospect receives your package is there a quick intake of breath, a delight . . . or a yawn?

Size

What's Better: Being in Shape or Being Out of Shape? Well, It Depends . . .

Envelopes, like people they go to, come in different shapes and sizes. Your choice, as a businessperson, should be limited to the more traditional sizes. Those you have in your drawer or your printer has in stock. There are usually three basic sizes. The small envelope (called the 6¾" commercial, which measures 6½" x 3⅝"), the big envelopes (called #10, they measure 9½" x 4⅛") and the 9" x 12" envelopes to mail papers you do not want folded.

As a businessperson, you can work with all three of these and have dozens of ways to make them not only more interesting and more readable, among the many envelopes that arrive and survive.

Each of the three basic envelopes can have a closed front *or* a small see-through window, through which the customer's name appears.

The Window Envelope

This has the advantage of not requiring typing the customer's name twice (once on the letter, again on the envelope). But the window has the disadvantage of not being a message that is close, personal, one-on-one. Which is why you see windows used so often by banks, insurance companies, government agencies. They have an "official" but distant appeal.

The Double Window Envelope

One of the windows has your name and address, the other has room for your imagination.

It could have the return name and address.

It could be a teaser message ("Your check for $100,000 . . .")

It could be a stamp or a drawing or another attention-getting idea. Good for sweepstakes, contests, giveaways ("Bring this in to win . . .").

Christmas Money Envelopes

These are the ones you ask your bank for at holiday time, to tuck in a dollar or more to give someone for a gift. When you open the envelope there is an oval cut-out showing a picture of the President on the money.

How about a picture of . . . yourself?

How about the giant word "free" so the reader has to reach inside and take out the entire message to see what *is* free? How about a giant "50% off" so the reader has to reach inside and take out . . . etc.

How about "Sale" or "Just for You" or "Discount Days" or "Exclusive" or . . . your choice of a word, statement, idea or gimmick so the reader has to reach inside and . . . well, you get the idea.

Check with your bank where *they* buy these envelopes and buy a batch for your next mailer.

The outside of the envelope says, *"Free Money for You."* And when you lift up the flap you see a familiar face looking at you through an oval cut-out. When you pull the complete mailer you see the money is a 76¢ coupon for our Washington's Birthday Sale.

Note: These are stock envelopes available through an envelope supply house. You might be familiar with them as available from your bank at Christmas bonus time.

Zip-opener Envelopes

If the key to successful direct mail is audience involvement (and it is), how do you make them become involved from the moment they receive the envelope? Here's one way: They open the envelope by pulling a tag on one side. That gets them inside and . . . reading.

What Does the Stationery Store Stock?

The tan-colored Kraft envelopes come in all the standard sizes described earlier but have a different "feel" and look. There are string and button closures for envelopes in stock. Or metal-clasp envelopes.

Visit the stationery store. Ask to see the different shapes and sizes they have in regular stock that are used by businesses other than yours.

What is an ordinary envelope for a different business will have an extra-ordinary look when you mail it to your customers.

Odds to Achieve the Ends . . .

And how about the odd-shaped envelope or carrier for your message?

Every day between 7:30 and 9:00 A.M. at our local post office, there is always a group of business and professional men and women who pick up their mail and sort it before they leave. Day after day, we watch them make a pile on the counter of the mail they will take back to the office with them. The rest they throw in a nearby wastebasket. The vast majority of this throw-away mail has something in common: it is two dimensional. The width and length may vary, but the thickness will be about the same.

See for yourself. Check your business direct mail this week. Chances are most, if not all, is two dimensional.

Recognizing the "sameness" of so many direct mail efforts—two dimensional look-alikes—you'll see a simple change in size will set your piece apart from the crowd.

An odd-shaped box. An extra-large envelope. A tube. That which is different from the norm attracts attention.

And yes, costs more . . .

If you are selling a product, the question is, "Will the additional sales offset the increased cost of the package and improve overall profit?" If you are seeking leads, you must decide whether or not the extra costs have generated enough leads to reduce your cost/lead. If you are soliciting contributions, not only will the odd-shaped mailing be expected to improve the returns, but it should also increase the dollar amount of the contributions received.

If you are selling executive jets to corporate presidents, you can well afford a more expensive package. If you are soliciting funds from your local college alumni association members, the package should be unusual and/or familiar enough to make them want to read but not so expensive as to cut into profits.

The size of your audience (mailing list) also affects the economics of your mailing. Frequently, the larger the mailing, the lower the cost for the package.

Now, put yourself in the post office at 8:30 A.M. on a Monday morning. Your mail contains a tube resembling a firecracker. The copy on the outside says "Here's a dynamite idea for your next sales meeting." You shake it and you hear something inside. Into the wastebasket unopened?

Never!

Tease for Two

Should you write "teaser" copy on the outside of your envelope?
Sure. Maybe. Sometimes. Never. Of course. Are you out of your mind?
All of which are correct answers.

Sure. When you send a letter to a consumer (not an executive). This front-page headline gives them a reason to keep on reading. Wanting to know more information is legitimate, to be desired and works. *Remember:* This sentence must *always* be your prime benefit and offer. One that is instantly understandable. Or—one that teases them into opening your envelope.

Maybe. If the headline offer does *not* give the reader a reason for reading and/or opening the envelope, it may do the exact opposite of what you want, and the envelope is thrown away. Make sure your outside teaser message promises a benefit or provokes curiosity.

Sometimes. Send some of your envelopes out with a message. Send some *without* a message. Code the inside return envelope or the coupon or response card so you know which pulls best. Next time use the one that worked best. But test again. Next time try a *different* message.

Never. Very personal business-to-business correspondence. Because teasers are not sophisticated, upscale, or business-looking. Too strong a sell turns many businesspeople off. We're not talking of magazine subscription letters or seminar notices. We're talking of the important message that demands the quiet confidentiality of a plain envelope.

Of course. The envelopes with the greatest response rate, award-winners (not trophies, but results) seem to be the ones with a message on the outside of the envelope. Why not copy the winners?

Are you out of your mind? An invitation to an opening of the new Rolls-Royce showroom, a letter from the Governor's Mansion or the White House. Or, simply, a personal letter from you to your customer.

The Massage of a Message

When you visit the local health club, the masseur gives you a massage which makes you more receptive to rest and response. How do we have your message massage your reader? Here are a few ways that have worked in the past that you can adapt and adopt for your own:

Start a story. The outside of the envelope has a message that continues on the *back* of the envelope that continues *inside* the envelope. Make sure this is interesting and the customer wants to know more.

Ask a question. There is a true/false quiz on the outside of the envelope and the answer is *inside* the envelope. Curious?

Use the back. People *do* turn envelopes over. But few have anything written on the back. Give the reader *another* reason to keep on reading.

Make it personal. Yes, you can put "Private and Confidential" on the outside of your envelope because you know the message will then go directly to the person involved. But, make sure the message *is* "Personal and Confidential," or the angry reader will toss it aside and remember your message did *not* live up to its statement! Bad news for your future mailings.

If you are sending mail to a business executive remember that typed names outpull labels.

Make it known. Leaving your name off the envelope may create a certain amount of curiosity. And some curiosity seekers will open the envelope. On the other hand, there are many who will think it merely a piece of advertising mail and toss it aside. Remember one of the reasons mail is read when it goes to your customer is that they know you. (See Chapter 3: The Five Ways Advertising Works.)

Your customers want to read about a product they own, the store where they shop, the newest merchandise they buy from *you.* So put your name out front for them to see.

Just a matter of timing. Setting a time limit is one of the "musts" of direct mail. Saying it up front draws attention to the fact. ("Only six more days till . . .")

Stamp of approval. Third class mail *usually* pulls as well as first class mail at about one-half the price. (See TOOLBOX on printed indicia). Metered postage will *usually* pull the same amount of business as putting on stamps.

Stamps do attract attention if they are foreign, a big assortment, or on a personal invitation. Even better if they tie into your theme, promotion or event.

The End Is the Same as the Beginning

If the outside envelope is the reason for *reading* then an inside envelope is the reason for *acting*. Tucking a reply envelope will increase a response whether it is a collection letter, a cash-with-order letter, or a "charge it" offer. Making your envelope postage paid will increase returns. (Exception: When you enclose an envelope with monthly statements, don't pay the return postage. Your return will be almost the same because people know they have to pay bills.)

Telling someone to come to your place of business for a sale or a special does *not* need a response envelope. An invitation with limited seating for a special event *does* need a response envelope.

So if your customer is asking for more information, placing the order through the mail, opening the account at the bank, sending in the first month's premium, filling out the orders for the books, he or she needs an envelope to complete the order, so enclose a postage-paid one.

Make it a business-reply pre-addressed envelope. This means you pay the postage when you are receiving the order. Would you pay a quarter for every customer who walks into your place of business ready to buy? Oh, yes.

Make the return envelope a different color. It stands out in the package and the customer won't toss it aside thinking that it was the outside envelope.

Conclusion

The envelope is the *outer* shell of your message.

Your job is to make it more attractive, more interesting, more eye-appealing than all the other envelopes received in the morning mail by your customer.

But no matter how attractive, interesting or eye-appealing your envelope is, the *inside* must be attractive, interesting and eye-appealing as well.

If your offer, your copy, your list, your design and all the other ingredients are not appealing, the greatest envelope in the world would be the same as the baby's rattle that is ripped apart to find out what's inside and the disappointment that comes even when you see there's nothing exciting inside that warranted all the noise.

TOOLBOX

The Postage

Most of the time you will send your mailing piece one of two ways, first class or third class mail.

First class mail is the way you usually send mail. You put a stamp in the upper right hand corner or run it through your postage meter machine.

If your mailing is an invitation, extremely personal or simply a small list (under 500) you can use first class mail and a postage stamp.

If your mailing is a selling piece and your list is 1,000 or more, you should consider printed indicia.

They look like this:

Bulk Rate
U.S. Postage
P A I D
Permit No. 63
Linwood, N.J.
08221

Here's how to save your own printed indicia: Visit your post office. (See Chapter 15.) Talk to the person who can give you information on third class mail. There is an annual fee for the right to use this printed box on your mailing. But there is a considerable savings in money (about one-half the postage) for you because you save the post office money.

Your mailings must be sorted by zip code and tied in bundles. (The exact how-to-do-it rules will be given you by the post office).

There is also a delayed delivery with third class mail so plan your mailings accordingly. First class mail leaves the post office as quickly as possible, Third class mail waits a while.

Here's what we do when we send out our mailings.

We contact the postmasters of *each* of the zip codes where our mailings go. We send them a copy of the mailer and a letter. In the letter we ask them to watch for our mailing coming to their post office because it is dated material. (Example: a sale.) The mail must be delivered on or before a certain date. If they do not have our mailing in their post office at least a week ahead of time, will they please call us? Thanks . . .

And then *we call them* a week ahead of time to make sure the mailing *did* arrive.

We have found this very effective, and the post office is usually very willing to work with you to make sure your mailing does go out on time.

Address Correction Requested

One out of five people in your community moves every year. Some are born. Some die. Some move in. Some move out. That means 20 percent of your mailing list *changes* every year.

The post office will cooperate with you in "cleaning" your list (making sure the addresses are accurate). Here's what you do. Put the phrase "Address Correction Requested" at the bottom of your envelope or mailer. This tells the letter carrier if the person no longer lives at the address then the post office will return the piece to you *with the corrected address*.

The post office will do this for about a year after the person has moved so it is important for you to "clean" your lists *at least* once a year. Put the phrase on *every* mailing so the changes do not become overwhelming at the end of every year.

There *is a* small charge for the post office giving you this information. It is worth the cost! Otherwise too many of your mailing pieces are simply sent to the wrong place, and the person you wanted to receive the notice does not.

Creative Envelope Formats

The double window envelope. All kinds of uses for this technique. This is one example. One window has the name and address of the sendee. The other window gives you a what-do-you-want-to-do option.

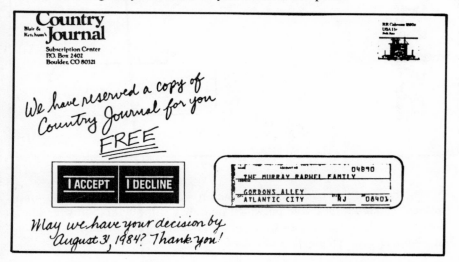

Note: This campaign *must* be working. We've received this exact same envelope for the past three years. The only change is the year.

The over-print envelope. A strong word or call to action overprinted on the envelope is another sure-fire way to gain attention and make the reader curious about what's inside.

Provoke curiosity. Ballot? Ballot for what? Is it voting time?
If you time this envelope to arrive at about voting time, it will create immediate attention on the part of the reader.

BALLOT

Please indicate your vote
on the enclosed ballot
and return it within 10 days

BLK. RT.
U.S. POSTAGE
PAID
Permit 40473

RUCG
MURRAY R. ADV
1012 ATLANTIC AVENUE
ATLANTIC CITY, NJ 08401

The ballot inside could be their vote on what they like best about your business (a survey). A vote on which item they will buy first on your sale. A vote on which items they want to see added to your inventory. A vote on whatever your imagination thinks of . . .

Can you come up with the answer? This award-winning envelope was designed by the creative team of Jayme-Ratalahti for *Esquire* magazine. What it does: has the reader become *involved* with the mailer. Which is the first step to have them read it.

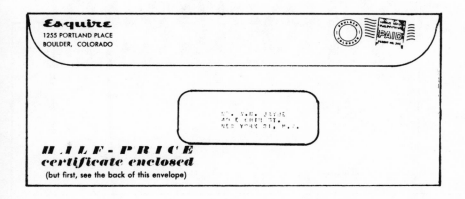

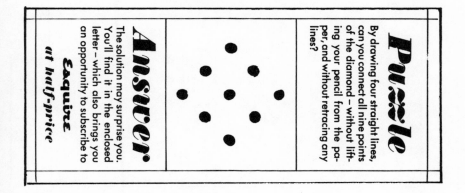

(If you can't come up with the answer, drop us a line, we'll send it to you . . .)

Gotcha coming & going. In this envelope for the Agatha Christie Mystery Collection, the Jayme-Ratalahti collaborators capture your interest in the front by asking if you know "Whodunnit," by offering a free . . . something. And extending you an "invitation to a murder."

Then, when you turn over the envelope, you have still *another* selling message asking you to come see how the other half . . . *dies.*

The sentence is printed in black but the "X" and word "dies' are printed in red.

Third-party subscriptions. Instead of a magazine asking you to sub- scribe or an insurance company asking you to buy its policies, they will often work with a prestigious and established institution to ask you to subscribe or buy.

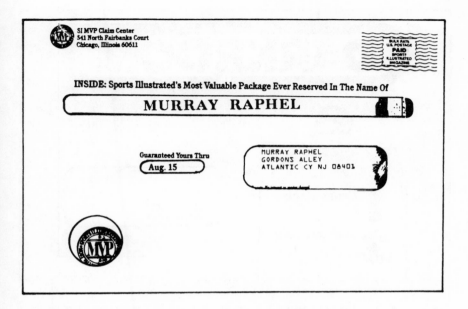

That was the case with this invitation from Neiman-Marcus department store offering the reader a discount on the sophisticated *Arts & Antiques* publication.

The headline, written by Bill Jayme, makes you wonder, What is this all about?

"This is either a forgery or a madly clever original."

Bulk Rate
U.S. Postage
Paid
Art & Antiques

An Invitation from

Neiman Marcus

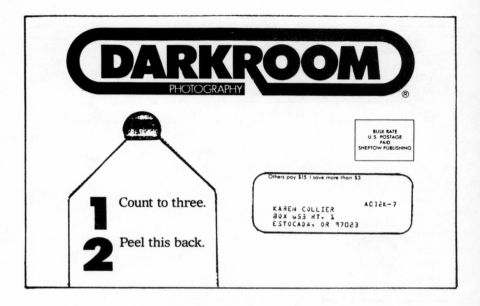

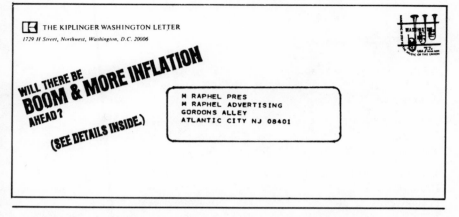

The Non-envelope envelope, we mention this earlier but it's worth repeating, suppose, just suppose, that instead of an envelope your mailing arrives in a box, or tube, or bag, or padded envelope. Who's brave enough to throw this piece in the wastebasket?

Naturally, what's inside the box, tube, bag, etc., has to be a cost consideration. It might be an advertising specialty, a sample, a gift, or even just the standard letter, brochure and business reply card (disguised). But it's a sure thing that your piece will be opened. Another variation is the odd shape or size envelope with unusual thickness or weight. Here's a story about a business-to-business mailer who took advantage of an odd size, shape and weight package.

A fabricator of stamped metal parts wanted to try direct mail to increase his customer base. But his services, prices, facilities and delivery were not much different from those of hundreds of other local metal fabricators. He needed to attract attention. His piece arrived in a large brown envelope, and it was heavy. Considering the additional postage, it had to be important (a small price to pay for a guaranteed opening). Inside the envelope was a letter and a business reply card. But the letter was silk screened on a piece of anodized aluminum. The letter had a headline that started off with the word "Look." The centers of the O's in Look had been punched out. And other portions of the letter had been punched. The copy explained that punching any size, quantity and shape holes in metal pieces was the company's specialty—and they did it with precision accuracy (just look at the close registration of the holes in the word Look).

Vive la Différence! The fabricator attracted attention that got the letter opened; the unique letter on an actual metal part got the letter read and the accompanying business reply card got the action (requests for quotations he desired.) Sure, it was an expensive piece, but the package was right, the offer was right and the audience was right and the first order from the first new customer proved that the cost of the package was really right. He won the battle of the wastebasket.

Envelope Sources

Atlantic Envelope Company
P.O. Box 1267
Atlanta, GA 30301

Automated Packaging Systems, Inc.
8400 Darrow Road
Twinsburg, OH 44087

The B & W Press, Inc.
100 Lynn Street
Peabody, MA 01960

Berlin & Jones Envelope Co., Inc.
2. E. Union Street
East Rutherford, NJ 07070

Boise Cascade Envelopes
72 Cascade Drive
Rochester, NY 14614

Design Distributors, Inc.
45 E. Industry Ct.
Deer Park, NY 11729

Double Envelope Corporation
7702 Plantation Rd. N.W.
Roanoke, VA 24019

Federal Envelope Company
660 Forbes Blvd.
S. San Francisco, CA 94080

Golden State Envelopes
1601 Gower Street
Los Angeles, CA 90028

Gotham Envelope Corp.
100 Avenue of Americas
New York, NY 10013

Heco Envelope
5445 N. Elston Avenue
Chicago, IL 60630

Karolton Envelope
209 E. 56 Street
New York, NY 10022

Mail-Well Envelope Company
P.O. Box 765
Houston, TX 77001

Specialty Envelope Company
4890 Spring Grove Avenue
Cincinnati, OH 04232

Tension Envelope Corp.
19th & Campbell Streets
Kansas City, MO 64108

Transo Envelope Company
3542 N. Kimball Avenue
Chicago, IL 60618

U.S. Envelope
P.O. Box 3300
Springfield, MA 01101

13
I've Got You on My List

WE VISITED A NEARBY supermarket that needed more sales. We asked if they had a mailing list. They said no.

We asked if they kept names of customers from contests, sweepstakes and in-store continuity programs. They said no.

We then asked if they issued courtesy cards so customers could cash checks.

"Sure."

Well, we asked, "isn't that a mailing list?"

"No," they answered. That was only the names of their courtesy card holders . . .

What happened?

The store *had* a mailing list and did not know they did. This situation is not uncommon. Most businesses have lists of customers on their charge accounts. They have names and addresses of best customers kept by sale people. They have alteration tags, layaways, call-back records, quotations, special order books and service calls. The problem is . . . no one thinks of these names as anything but . . . names.

But they are something far more important. They are names of the people who know you, buy from you and are interested in what you have to say/sell to them in the future. They are the nucleus of your very own data base. Your mailing list.

Let us tell you up front, now, before we go any further, THE LIST is one of the two must-have ingredients for successful direct mail. (We put it in capital letters. That means it is important.)

So you are not kept in suspense, we'll drop the other shoe, which is called "The Product or Service." (Remember that: It was Chapter 4.)

Now. Today. At once. Begin your mailing list.

169

Think of all the places you have customers names. Start with the ones we mentioned a few paragraphs above.

Put these names, addresses and zip codes on 3″ x 5″ cards in a little box. Let them accumulate. You will see they will quickly multiply as the days go by. Soon a few hundred names become a few thousand.

☐ **YES,** I want to receive mail from Gordon's.

Mr/Mrs/Ms_____
       First name   Middle initial   Last name

Permanent

Address_____

_____

City_____State_____Zip_____

Home Phone(___)_____Business Phone(___)_____

If you have a service or professional business or if you are a wholesaler, your clients are your mailing list.

If you have a store, print up 3″ x 5″ "I want to receive mail from . . ." paper slips. Very simple. Very inexpensive. Place them on all your check-out counters. Do not worry about the cashier(s) taking a lot of time gathering all this information at check-out time. They don't. Here's how it works:

Your customer brings her package to the check-out counter. Your cashier says, "We have a special mailing list. It is only for our regular customers. Just fill this out and you'll receive some exciting notices we mail only to special people like you . . ."

They will almost tear the pen out of the cashier's hand in their hurry to sign. Everyone wants to be "in the know." You want to offer them something no one else knows about and are they interested?

Oh, yes.

Gathering names is habit-forming, just like eating peanuts. Once you start you will find you cannot stop. But you have to *start*. You have to set the example yourself and others in your business will follow. Ask everyone at the end of the day. "How many people did we [you?] sign on our mailing list today?"

At this early stage do not worry if someone signs up twice. You will catch their name later. (We'll show you how.)

Right from the start, you might want to be a little more sophisticated in your name gathering. Perhaps you have a checklist on your sign-up list of what they are buying. Women's merchandise. Men's. Children's. A list of people buying a particular brand. We have a list of names of customers who buy only one designer's clothing. We mail them something *every* month just from this designer. Our return averages 20 percent! The per unit sale is more than $100. Very effective. We simply added this designer's name to the sign-up list.

If the customer bought this merchandise, we checked it off at the point of sale on the list they filled out.

Remember this simple rule: If a customer spends money with you, his name goes on the mailing list.

Not the shoppers and browsers and let's-kill-some-time-here folks. The ones who actually spend: They are customers.

Definition of a customer: Someone who spends one dollar with you at least one time in your store or business. Now your customer may also be a customer of your competition. But he knows who you are and has shown enough faith to spend his money at least once.

This is the customer you want. Because (and here's our theme song you've heard repeated over and over again throughout this book), "Dollar for dollar nothing will return as much business to you as direct mail." Because . . .

'TIS FAR, FAR EASIER TO SELL MORE TO THE CUSTOMER YOU HAVE THAN TO SELL A NEW CUSTOMER.

If that's true (and it is) then how do we have that customer come back and back and back and back *ad profitum?*

We could advertise in the newspaper and radio and TV and magazines and church bulletins. But that's advertising to *everyone.* We want you to advertise to *someone.* That someone whose name you now have on your *list.*

O.K., you've started. You put out slips for people to sign up for your list. (Or you have typed up a client list coded with the kind of product or service the customer uses from your business.) You assign someone to go over any area of your business that might have customers' names and addresses. You copy those on your 3" x 5" cards. File the cards alphabetically. Easier to look up and see whether or not a new name is listed twice.

You can maintain your own list for a few thousand names. You are now ready to (choose one):

1. Write or type labels for small mailings.
2. Write or type up envelopes from names and addresses on cards.

When the list grows bigger, contact a local mailing house. They will put all your names on a computer for you and print labels or the name directly on your mailing piece.

They will print your names. And/or they will code the names when they put them in the computer so if you want just *certain* names to mail to certain people who buy just certain merchandise or use a certain service, fine!

You checked off that information on the original sign-up list, remember? Now, you tell your mailing house to simply pull only these names. The computer is smart. If you told the computer in the beginning about those names, they will tell you back.

The mailing house also performs a service called Merge & Purge. Sounds like a South American coup. What it really is: computers have a way of "scanning" each new name they receive. If it "looks" the same as one they already have with the same address, they simply "purge" that name out . . . all the while they are "merging" the other names in.

But that's down the road.

First: collect the names. Count them. Do you have 1,000? Great. Time to start.

Here's why: Dr. Russell Conwell gave a speech called "Acres of Diamonds" more than 100 years ago. The theme: Why are you trying so hard to find new places to make your fortune when the fortune is waiting right in your own backyard?

The speech was so much in demand, he told and retold it thousands of times throughout the United States eventually making more than $6 million which he used to found Temple University in Philadelphia, Pennsylvania.

What was he saying? This: If you want your sales to increase, if you want your business to grow, if you want more ringings of your register, practice a proven, successful and winning formula called, *Keep In Touch* which, for the purpose of this chapter, we condense to the initials KIT.

Think about it.

If you have a bank, and customers have a checking account, why don't they have a savings account? And if they have a checking and savings account, why not an IRA? And if they have a checking and savings account, and an IRA, why not a loan? And if they have a checking and savings account, an IRA, and a loan, why not . . . well, you get the idea.

If you have a supermarket, you know your average customer spends about $30 a week with you. And, therefore (say you), they cannot spend anymore. Makes sense, until you see the same customer coming out of a nearby convenience store with another bag of groceries. These are not only the same groceries you have in your store, but they are groceries that could cost more in the convenience store.

If you have a clothing store you know what your customers can afford to spend, based on their past experience with you, their job, and the size of their family. And you are content to have a good triple figure sale at the beginning of a season. You conclude that they spend as much as they can afford. Until you see them come out of another store in the nearby shopping mall with another shopping bag full of clothing you sell in your store.

The ancient Roman philosopher Prato was the first to tell us about the 80-20 rule. (Remember that one? Let's have a show of hands from those who remember. Good!) Prato said 80 percent of your sales are brought to you by only 20 percent of your customers. Fund raisers for major political campaigns or charity drives say, "Yes, we want a lot of names to establish the bandwagon approach."

"Everybody's contributing. Don't you want to be among the bunch?"

But their real effort, their intense drive, their pinpoint marketing is keyed to the much, much smaller group (the 20 percent) who wind up giving the lion's share (80 percent) of the money.

Sometimes the figures are even more dramatic than that. Roger Horchow in his book *Elephants in Your Mailbox* writes about his business in 1974 when "the rent-payers were ten customers who were spending over $10,000 a year with us."

Competition gets tougher as new products, ideas, stores spring up around you; remember, if business is good, it's because you are buying well and selling well. It's because you are doing something right.

And if business is bad, it's not the weather. It's not the economy. It's not the location. It's you. You are doing something wrong—because somebody is buying something somewhere. Your job is to figure out how to have customers spend a larger part of their disposable dollars in your store, buying your merchandise.

This philosophy is best practiced by a major association of meat packers. This association says that a stomach has only so much capacity— say 32 ounces. The goal of the packers is for meat to take up as many of those ounces as possible.

The goal of your business is to capture as many of those dollars as possible. And you have the KIT to do it.

The reason KIT works is that your customers want to hear from you. They shop your business. They spend their money with you. They trust you. Your letter in the mail, your voice over the phone is familiar, comfortable, easy. People like you do things from habit. Of course, there are the adventurers who want to vacation in a different city every year.

But there are far more who buy the second home or condominium in a familiar place because they are "comfortable" there. People are uncomfortable in a new place or strange surroundings. Doctors tell us when patients wake up from an operation they do not say, "Who am I?" they say, "Where am I?" Everyone wants to be familiar, comfortable, at home. (See Chapter 3, Give Me Five!)

And your customers feel that way in your place of business. If something happens with your business and they are not informed, they are resentful. It's like a friend telling secrets and leaving you out. You get mad. That is what happened to Roger Bailey, a bank officer in Grand Island, Nebraska.

He writes: "We sent an extensive mailing to customers advertising our ATM (Automatic Teller Machines). One was inadvertently sent empty— the addressed envelope but nothing inside. The customer called and asked what was in the envelope. After all, if it came from her bank, it must be important.

"I apologized, explained the brochure and thought that ended the conversation. I was wrong. The customer insisted I send the brochure anyway. She wanted to see what she missed from her bank . . ."

What all this proves is that your customers care. They want to know. They will respond to your calling or writing, your KIT.

And so when business is off and sales are down and you stare at the front doors wondering when the next customer will come in, start planning on what you will do today to let your present customers know you are there to cherish, love, and full over them.

They're your list!

And you can pack up your troubles in your old KIT bag and smile, smile, smile.

TOOLBOX

We said it in this chapter, we've mentioned it in other chapters, but it can't be said too often: 'If you have a record of your customers' names and addresses you already have your most important mailing list. Remember, *'tis far, far easier to sell more to the customer you have than to sell a new customer."*

Prospect List

Your next best list is your prospect list. What's a *prospect?* A prospect is someone who has shown an interest in your products or services but who has not yet bought (she may be a *customer* for one item but a *prospect* for another.) It seems every day someone in one of our offices makes a phone call for quotations on a wide variety of products or services. We're always amazed at how few of the people we call ask, "Who are you?" Who we are is a *prospect.*

Rented Lists

A list broker once told me if I needed a list of left-handed golfers he could get it for me.

First thought: "Wow!"

Second thought: It probably isn't too difficult. Find a manufacturer of custom golf clubs and rent his customer list of lefties.

That's how it is with lists. They're available for almost any specific kind of prospective buyer. You name the audience and there's a list. (It's been estimated that there are over 50,000 lists.)

Where do these lists come from?

People who have customer lists often rent them—either directly to you or through list brokers.

Where do you find the people who rent these lists?

First stop: the classified section of your telephone directory under the heading "Mailing Lists." Here you'll find not only sources for national lists but also sources for local lists and names of firms who will help you maintain your own lists.

Next . . . get a copy from the library (or buy a copy) of *Standard Rate & Data Service* (SRDS) *Guide to Consumer Mailing Lists* (3004 Glenview Road, Wilmette, IL 60091. Phone: 1-800-323-4601.) This book has pages and pages of listings of almost all available lists with detailed information about each list.

Borrowed Lists

Trade publications sometimes let their advertisers borrow their sub-scribers list. They won't actually *give* you the names for you to use but will ask you to furnish *them* with *your* mailing.

They will address and mail, charging you for the postage. People are *very* fussy about who actually sees their list.

You might also try swapping lists with a friendly business that does not have competitive products or services. We have helped several clients by putting them together for list swaps.

Compiled Lists

These are lists of names and addresses of people or firms without respect to whether or not they ever bought anything by mail. Typically they could be lists from local or state governments, lists from directories, or automobile owners lists (in states where their sale is still legal).

The Different Ways to Keep Your Mailing List (Advantage/ Disadvantage)

3" x 5" cards
• For up to about 500 names.
• Inexpensive.
• Easy to check for duplicate names or addresses.
But . . .
• Each name has to be typed each time.
• Best for first class mailings.

Labels
• For about 1,000 to 2,000 names.

- Inexpensive.
- Easy to add names

But . . .

- Difficult to find duplicate names
- Mailings have to be arranged in zip code order
  (Which you *can* do instead of by alphabet, but that presents other problems like *finding* the name.)

*Computer**

- For about 3,000 to 5,000 names or more.
- Inexpensive to add names.
- Easy to check on duplicates.
- Computer can do other things: write letters, keep track of accounts.
- Can rearrange names for zip coding.

But . . .

- It's expensive.
- Requires good planning.
- Takes a lot of time to delete names (in comparison to the ways above).
- You better have back-up material, just in case something happens to the information on the computer disk.

Lettershop

- Work done by someone else. Doesn't disturb your normal routine.
- Mailing goes from printer to post office.

But . . .

- Costs more.
- You don't have the tight control over your mailer.
- Sometimes you have to wait for your mailings until they take care of a bigger customer.

---

*This refers to your own in-house computer. When your list gets over 5,000, contact mailing service companies to do this work for you.

14
It May Look Like a Computer But It's Really a Cash Register

PROBABLY THE MOST significant change in direct mail in recent years has been the computer—particularly the inexpensive personal computer.

Now it's possible for the smallest direct mailer to maintain his own list with the ability to print addresses or labels.

The computer with appropriate software can be used as a word processor to write copy, or to personalize letters, or to file and store test results for mailings and referred to at the touch of a key. Like its many other applications, the computer has dramatically changed our ability to produce more effective direct mail. If your business already has a computer, you can adapt the equipment you use for other purposes to direct mail.

For others, the big problem is the selection of appropriate equipment and software. What should you buy? How much should you spend? Veterans of this selection process warn that the software decision should come before the hardware decision.

Ask yourself: What do you want your computer to do?

A careful analysis must be made to determine what you want to accomplish:

- How much information do you want to store?
- In how many varied forms?
- How fast do you need to retrieve this information?
- How many people need access to the equipment?
- And when?
- What about budget?

These are all questions to answer *before* you make the decision for both software and hardware.

Considering the tremendous variety of equipment and programs available, the best help on what to buy is from other business friends who use computers for direct mail. (Good place to start: a meeting of your nearest direct mailing club. See Appendix I, Join the Club.) If you cannot get adequate help from a reputable dealer, try a consultant.

The small consulting fee will save you large financial mistakes.

Let's look at some effective uses of the computer for your direct mail program.

Mailing Lists

Your best customers are your current customers. With the computer you can maintain a mailing list of customers each time you produce an order or write a quotation or send a bill.*

You can also build a list of prospects by adding names picked up from other sources.

The computer, with the right software, allows you to *segment* your mailing list. Example: You are a manufacturer of electronic parts. You can code and recall purchasing names, engineering names and management names. Retailers might code on a "last time bought" basis and call up those names of people who have not made recent purchases. A video store might segment according to a viewers *tastes*.

Best of all, segmentation is not limited to one function. You can build in multiple variables to further refine your audience.

Addressing

Having selected the names you want to use, your computer is now ready for addressing. You have the option of address labels or of individually addressing letters and envelopes from the names stored in memory.

Customers and businesses are familiar with mailing labels. Label addressing is almost always as effective as typewritten or stencil addressing. Exception: An envelope to a business executive should have a typewritten name on the envelope, not a label.

For smaller, highly personalized letters (remember direct mail is a *personal* medium), you can enter individual names into stock letters stored in the memory of a computer.

Important: Yes, your computer can "drop" the person's name throughout the letter and it becomes a high form of personalization. But you can

---

*Computers help you keep accurate information on three marketing statistics: Recency, Frequency and Monetary. *Recency:* How often they buy. *Frequency:* The average number of purchases or responses per year. *Monetary:* How much they spend. Per order. Per year.

have a *personalized* letter that is not a *personal* letter. There *is* a difference. The worst crime in letter writing is to make a personal letter sound impersonal because of over-personalization.

Tests have shown that many readers *resent* too much personalization. You've seen those letters. The ones that tell you what street you live on, the make of your car and the school your child goes to every day. This is a turn-off to many customers. They feel Orwell and Big Brother have arrived in the morning mail.

And the most personal letter is the least personal letter if the name is misspelled. The daily mail is filled with letters and packages to Endman, Herdman, Erman, Ratfeld, Rapehel, Rafel and more . . . If you begin your "personal" letter with "Dear Erdman, Kenneth B.," we never make it to the opening sentence.

Word Processing

If you are writing your copy in house, the word processing capabilities of your computer are invaluable for both time savings and accuracy. The ability to constantly review and make changes on the screen before printing is a definite aid to creativity.

Testing

The computer offers a convenient way to store test information for future recall as the least of its test functions. Beyond that, when you get involved in more sophisticated testing, the computer will be the tool to solve mathematical problems and produce the statistical results you'll need.

When you put information on a computer, remember the formula: Garbage In, Garbage Out. What that means: If you put the wrong information into the computer, you will receive wrong information back. This is important when you spell names, enter addresses. But it is vital when you are putting in the zip code. A misplaced, forgotten or transposed number simply makes your mailing piece ineffective because it just doesn't get there . . .

In his introduction to *But Would Saks Fifth Avenue Do It?* publisher Pete Hoke of *Direct Marketing* magazine tells the story of Kermit Goldberg from Baltimore, Maryland.

"He had installed an IBM Systems III for inventory control. That problem solved, he worried about how else to use the machine. One of Kermit's constant concerns over the years was the logic of huge sale ads in newspapers. Wasn't this a public announcement that the merchant had bought too much, or the wrong merchandise? Didn't sale advertising make some customers wonder why they should buy at regular prices? Did the sale really move the merchandise out?

Kermit woke up one night with a great idea. What if, he mused, What if I put the suit size of every sale on my new computer? He did so the next day. In a year, he had his answer. Experience had shown that if he had ten 43 longs left after the season, he would need to select only sixteen people off the file who had bought 43 longs. A simple computer message sent to those sixteen, inviting each individual to come into the store the following week to buy another suit at 20 percent off, would sell the ten suits. That's a 60 percent response! And at a cost of about $7. And no city-wide announcement of Clearance, Clearance, Clearance at full page newspaper rates."

Is that direct mail? Sure. Highly selective? Of course! And just one application of the medium.

Remember, it may look like a computer, but when properly used it will work like a cash register ringing up those extra sales.

The two major uses of computers for small businesses doing direct mail are (1) mailing list storage, and (2) word processing. Those functions consist of . . .

• *Correcting, editing, updating:* You can make corrections as you are typing. You can store all the information and bring it up on the computer screen at a future date adding, subtracting, changing the information you have stored.

• *Selecting.* You can bring up certain names and addresses without going through the entire list (see examples that follow).

• *Calculating.* You have a built in math department that adds, subtracts, multiplies, divides for you.

• *Storing.* You have all the information you want or need on a paper thin *disc* instead of books, papers and bulky files.

• *Merging:* You have some new, up-to-date information. This can be *merged* into the material you already have.

TOOLBOX

What about computers for mailing lists? Good idea. But the number of small businesses in the U.S. (that's you) that do keep a data base (a list of customers, names who respond to ads, names of prospects in directories, referrals, in person, on the phone) is only about 400,000. That may seem like a lot but not really when you measure it against the *6 million businesses* in this country.

So . . . if you need a computer for a word processor and/or need a computer for a mailing list, fine.

The other TOOLBOX sections in this book tell you specifically how to do what we wrote about.

In this section on computers, we want to tell you when *not* to do it.

Computers are the buzzword of today's business. But unless they serve a need for you and your business, the word may really be to buzz off . . .

Most people cannot tell you what they really want to do in their lifetime. But most can tell you what they really do *not* want to do. And so, do *not* consider computers if your mailing is . . .

• *Used rarely.* You decide to begin. You will send a notice of your twice-a-year sale. And maybe some kind of announcement in between. *Do not use a computer.*

• *Small list.* Your mailing list is a couple of hundred names. Keep the names on 3″ x 5″ cards. Or have them typed on address labels with three carbons by a local secretarial service. *Do not use a computer.*

Use computer printouts on monthly statements. Everyone closely examines their monthly statement to see if the balance is correct. Great place for high readership to remind customers of an upcoming sale, special hours or a new product. The cost is nothing since the computer simply prints it at the same time it prints the statement.

Note the example of the $250 in free fall clothing drawing. The top of the statement is the entry blank. Total returned to the store: 325 out of 1,500 mailed. Total dollars spent by these people: More than $5,000. Would some of those dollars be spent anyway? Yes. *But not all of them* . . .

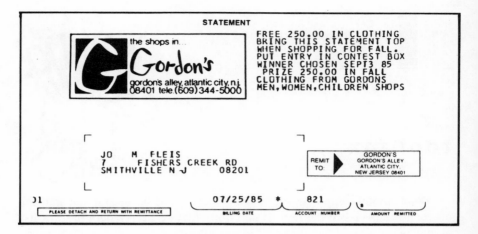

Special mailings for special customers. By using a code letter, you can break down your mailing list so the comptuer only prints the names you want.

If your customers only buy hardware, your computer will print address labels of hardware customers when you code them with an "H" (for hardware) or other identification symbol.

In the example above, these are mailings we sent out monthly to Polo clothing customers. We mail about 1,000 a month. Our cost—including postage and printing—is less than $500. Our average sales on these mailing pieces: About $5,000.

If you buy one product from a catalog, your name can be pulled out by computer for just that one product.

That is what 20 Century Plastics did in this letter to customers who only buy plastic sheets for slides or photos.

Also included was a catalog with different kinds of plastic sheets.

20TH CENTURY PLASTICS

August, 1988

Dear Preferred Customer:

You've shown your concern regarding proper storage and protection for your photographs with past purchases of 20th Century Plastics Photo Pages. These unique pages provide a convenient organizational system for all your slides, prints, and negatives.

Now you can stock up on all the pages and albums you need to organize summer photographs, create attractive product presentations, expand slide files, etc., AND receive a handsome Camera Bag for only $2.99 with your order! (See the enclosed coupon for details.) Just return the coupon with your order before November 30th to receive this versatile bag at this special low price!

The enclosed brochure describes all of our exclusive photo page styles—the largest selection available anywhere! And, with many of our page styles, you'll receive a Deluxe Album FREE! For that extra special touch, we can personalize your album in gold for only $1.50! (Details inside.)

Because we value you as our customer, we want to be certain that you're 100% satisfied with your order. If you're not, just return the merchandise within 30 days for a full refund.

It's easy to order! Just return the enclosed Order Form or call TOLL-FREE: 1-800-421-4662. We'll rush your order to you by return mail.

Sincerely,

Robert D. Shipp

Robert D. Shipp
President

P.S. Order your Photo Pages NOW to receive your valuable Camera Bag for only $2.99! This is a limited time offer...so place your order TODAY!

Note the added offer of the "camera bag for only $2.99" with your order. Great tie-in. Excellent way to have you buy the product in order to receive the bag. Remember "The Psychology of the Second Interest"? (See Chapter 4.)

PART THREE:

POSTING THE PACKAGE

15
Prescription for Profit: Make an Appointment With Your Postmaster

ONCE UPON A TIME a visit to the post office was an awesome trip. You entered a stone-cold building, spoke in hushed tones and were surrounded by pictures of the FBI's most wanted criminals. An infraction or mistake on your part could be a government offense punishable by fine or jail sentence . . . or both!

In 1970, the United States Post Office became the United States Postal Service. Everything changed. A quasi-governmental agency behaved more like a business than a government agency.

On a recent trip to our local post office (serves 7,000 customers), we found a modern lobby containing a display case promoting philatelic activities, a free-standing display called a "service information center," a "packaging pointers" poster, charts for fees and information, signs promoting Express Mail, racks with helpful hand-outs on postal products, and a repetitive electronic billboard with a lighted small-dots message promoting post office boxes.

Yes, there was a poster "conformity with signs and directions" that spelled out potential customer pitfalls and punishments.

All persons in and on property shall comply with official signs of a prohibitory or directory nature and with the directions of security force personnel or other authorized individuals. Violators subject to a $50.00 fine or 30-day jail sentence or both.

In spite of this ominous warning sign (even retailers post shoplifting warnings), post offices are looking and acting more like the retail business they really are. They merchandise their products and services. More importantly, they are servicing their customers. This new approach could save you, the mailer, untold wasted hours and money.

189

Even the so-called experts in direct mail, the mass mailers, make costly mistakes that could be avoided by a visit to their local post office *before* the mailing is produced. For the smaller do-it-yourself mailer an advance trip to the post office should be as important a safety measure as buckling up your seat belt when you get into your car.

Yes, there is printed material available from the Postal Service telling you what to do, how to do it and how much it will cost. But much is left out. Or subject to interpretation. Solution: Bring your proposed mailing to the postmaster (sometimes called superintendent) or other supervisory personnel. You gain the advice and help of experts. The post office would rather prevent problems than have to deal with them. They too believe in preventive medicine.

Here's some examples of very basic mailings. And what could (and did) go wrong.

The mailing	*The problem*
1. A self-mailer with a tear off business reply card.	1. The mailer was printed on paper stock too thin (or too light) for postcards.
2. A store mails an envelope with a letter brochure and business reply card. (BRC)	2. The letter, brochure, BRC so carefully weighed was weighed on a scale that did not agree with the post office "official" scale. Or it was weighed at the wrong time. (See Ken's rainy day mailer below.)
3. A business sent a package similar to the one above but included a specialty item which did *not* bring the package over the one ounce first class maximum.	3. The post office agreed the specialty did not add too much weight but said it *did* add too much *bulk* to permit the package to be mailed at the one ounce rate.

And then there are the not-so-common problems. We call them OOPS mail.

The Potato That Plopped

A creative sales manager of a manufacturer of cloth kitchen accessories came up with a unique direct mail package to promote a new line of oven barbeque mitts. In his package he included a letter, a descriptive catalog sheet and a sample of the mitt . . . along with a potato wrapped in aluminum foil positioned in the middle of the mitt.

The package was timed to capitalize on the spring selling season and was mailed in February. Unfortunately it was during one of the most severe cold spells in years. When many of the dealers opened what should have been a really exciting mailing, they were faced with potatoes that had frozen and then thawed, with mitt and literature stained at best and downright gooey at worst.

OOPS!

How to Unscramble an Egg

And then there was the time Murray came up with the after-Easter promotion. He would send a plastic egg out to his customers in a cloth bag. Inside the egg there would be a message about his store's after-Easter clothing sale. The mail was sent to 10,000 prime customers with the 10,000 messages tucked inside the 10,000 plastic eggs. The mailing label had the message, "Look what the Easter bunny left for you at Gordon's."

The day of the mailing, Murray took a dozen of the packages and gave them to some staff. He was anxious to see how they would open the eggs, what message they would read first.

Each of the salespeople opened the packages, took out the eggs, held them in their hands and said, "Thanks."

"Thanks?" echoed Murray, "Thanks for what?"

"For the plastic egg. Is this a gift you are sending to all your customers?"

"But," said Murray, "Aren't you going to open the egg?"

"Oh?" said one of the group, "does it open?"

And so Murray went to the local stationery store and purchased 10,000 peel-off dots and brought them to the printer. The printer stamped "Open me up" on the 10,000 dots. And the 10,000 packages were opened and the 10,000 eggs taken out and the label attached to each one and then re-packaged in the 10,000 bags.

P.S. The sale *was* a sucecss but came perilously close to being a candidate for the OOPS! parade.

Soak It to Me!

A mailing that Ken did (he got smart the hard way) was carefully designed to take maximum advantage of First Class weight limits. Accurate scales confirmed the weight—just a hair under one ounce—which allowed Ken to put a lot of material into the envelope. The promotion was mailed at the end of a rainy week in April. It was returned by the post office marked "insufficient postage." The paper had absorbed enough moisture to bring the weight of each piece over the one ounce mark.

OOPS!

Most mailings, with careful attention to planning and detail, will make it through the post office trouble free.

Your appointment at the post office is painless (and you won't get a bill). As with any organization, personal attitudes—the staff's bedside manner—may vary. We've found however that good patients can expect excellent care in the capable hands of the United States Postal Service.

TOOLBOX

Since postal regulations and rates are subject to change (and changes are planned even as this book is being written), only basic reference material is included in the TOOLBOX for this chapter.

Up-to-date information is available from your local post office supervisor. If your mailings turn out to be substantial, consider joining your local Postal Customer Council.

In addition to meetings, these local councils sponsor seminars, panels and classes. They focus on fundamentals of mail preparation, automation, Express Mail, presort first-class mail preparation and bulk mail. Many meetings feature national as well as local or regional speakers who are experts in the industry. At evening meetings you may have a special tour of the post office during its busiest hours. For a membership, call your local post office supervisor and ask for a membership application.

Two additional key sources for postal information, both free:

• *Mailers Guide*—a booklet covering basic service and procedures.

• *Memo to Mailers*—a monthly newsletter to keep you current with continuing postal changes.

Both publications are at your local United States Postal Service (USPS) or write to:

Memo to Mailers
c/o U.S. Postal Service Headquarters
Washington, D. C. 20260

Now, let's take a look at the different ways you can mail . . .

Classes of Mail

There are four basic classes of mail:

First Class. The basic category. More than half of the 106-plus billion pieces mailed annually are first class. For some types of mail (bills, statements of account, personal letters, etc.) it's the only method legally usable.

Remember, airmail? Well, it no longer exists as a special rate in the United States. USPS schedulers determine whether to use surface or air, depending on distance and weather.

Second Class. For newspapers and magazines with regular publication schedules.

Third Class. Commonly known as "bulk mail." Used for advertising that *must* be presorted by zip code. A single piece of Third Class mail has a maximum weight. This changes so check with your post office.

Fourth Class. Zone rated for parcels. *Special Fourth Class* is a flat rate by weight for books and sound recordings.

All the above are very simple explanations because most classes also have sub-classes.

Remember: these are the ones you will use most often. Postal rules and regulations change often. So check before you mail.

Something Extra—Express Mail. A premium overnight delivery service which is available to many (but not all) postal destinations.

In some instances where Express Mail cannot be delivered directly to the receiver, it can be delivered to the intended receiver's post office for pick up.

Authorizations and Permits

Imprint permit. A permit to use permit imprints and pay postage in cash at the time of mailing may be obtained on application to the post office where mailings will be made. There is a small one-time fee as long as the permit remains active.

Bulk rate annual fee. An annual bulk mailing fee must be paid once each calendar year (due January 1st) by or for any person or organization which mails at the regular or special bulk Third Class rates at each post office where mailings will be deposited.

The imprint and bulk rate indicia looks like this:

> Bulk Rate
> U.S. Postage
> **P A I D**
> Permit No. 63
> Linwood, N.J.
> 08221

This is the permit number your post office will issue especially for you.

This is the post office from which you will mail your mailers.

Business reply permit. If your direct mail package is going to include a pre-paid by you business reply card or envelope you will need a business reply permit. Currently, there are two ways to do this:

1. You can buy a $50 permit and pay $.47 each for reply, or,

2. Spend an additional $160 for a permit that requires only $.29 each reply.*

The decision is yours based on the anticipated returns.

Address corrections. Your mailer should have the words: ADDRESS

*Costs are as of 1985 and are used only for purposes of comparison.

CORRECTION REQUESTED or RETURN POSTAGE GUARANTEED or ADDRESS COR-
RECTION REQUESTED or FORWARDING AND RETURN POSTAGE GUARANTEED,
for you to receive new unchanged addresses.

Dimensions for mailing pieces. The USPS has strict regulations regarding all dimensions of mailing pieces for all classes of mail including width,
length, thickness of stock (postcards), thickness of total package and
weight. Check your mailing in advance to make sure it meets all the rules.

First Class vs. Third Class: Advantages/Disadvantages

First class mail . . .
- Has the fastest delivery.
- Requires no bundling or sorting.
- If person is not at address shown, you receive mail back (so you
  can take them off your mailing list).

But . . . it is the most expensive and costs jump dramatically as weight
increases.

Third class mail . . .
- Has the lowest cost per unit.
- Costs increase slowly as weight increases.

But . . . mailings must be pre-sorted and bundled by zip code.
- Delivery is the longest.
- Must have permit.
- You pay for finding out new addresses.

How to Make Sure Your Mailer Arrives on Time

Start at the beginning. Making sure your mailer arrives in the post
office *in time to be delivered* means making sure it is *ready* to arrive at the
post office in time.

Here's a timetable to follow. And the best way to plan ahead is to work
backwards. If that sounds confusing, it really is not. Because you have to
have certain things done at certain times.

1. What's the date of the "happening" in your mailer?
2. What is the date you want this mailer in your customer's hand?
3. What is the date you will deliver this mailer to your post office?
4. What is the date you will have it addressed and bundled?
5. What is the date you will have it printed?
6. What is the date you will have it delivered to the printer ready-to-
print?
7. What is the date you will establish what you want to accomplish and
what you want to spend?

. . . *That's the date to start from!*

Fact and Fiction About Your Post Office and Mail

Fact: Sending your mail early in the day means it will arrive at its destination earlier.

Fact: Most businesses waste money on postage. They "guess" what it should cost. So they put on too much postage. (waste of money) or too little and the mailer comes back (waste of time). Buy a small postage scale at your local stationery store. It will save you money.

Fact: "Next day" mail can arrive three days later. And be *on time,* according to the post office. Here's why: You did not check the last *pick-up* time at the mailbox. If it was 5 P.M. and you mail at 6 P.M., you lose a day. Or more on a weekend.

Fact: They respond to complaints. With more than 100 billion pieces of mail every year, something is bound to go wrong somewhere, sometime. Put your complaint in writing to the local postmaster. He will contact you (usually a phone call) with an explanation, help and advice.

Fact: First class mail is priced by the ounce. So it costs as much to mail something that only weighs an eighth of an ounce as something that weighs an ounce. Include a reminder sheet, an order blank, another offer . . . for the same postage. And/or work with your printer on using *lighter weight* paper for stationery and envelopes.

Fact: Business envelopes (#10) travel faster. Reason why: they are processed by machine.

Fact: If you're mailing first class, write it. Say so. Stamp it. Mark it. Especially on larger envelopes which are usually thought of as third class packages. Nothing wrong with writing "First Class Mail" real big on the envelope. Everyone wants to receive something that's First Class.

Fiction: The post office won't help you. Wrong. Forget the comedians' jokes. The post office will help you. Much of it is free. Ask for the booklet, *Mailer's Guide.* This answers more than you really want to know about every day questions. Their monthly newsletter, *Memo to Mailers* will keep you up to date with what's new.

One of the very best sources for what's happening in Washington, the source of all post office regulations, is John Jay Daly, President of Daly Associates, 702 World Center Building, 918 - 16th Street N.W., Washington DC 20006-2993. Write him for information on his Tipsheets and many small, informative and chock-full of facts postal and direct mail brochures. Tell him Murray and Ken sent you . . .

16
Testing, One, Two, Three. Is Anybody Really Listening?

WHICH OF THESE is the correct answer?

☐ A successful direct mail piece is one that has a return of 2 percent.

☐ A successful direct mail piece is one that has a return of 90 percent.

☐ A successful direct mail piece is one that has a return of one-half of one percent.

Answer: All of them.

How can that be?

Simple. It depends on what you are selling.

If you send out invitations to close friends, contractors, politicians, good customers and local suppliers to attend the grand opening of your new building and, if at this grand opening, you were going to have lavish refreshments, entertainment, door prizes and gifts, you might well expect close to 100 percent response.

If you are selling mainframe computers by mail, one lead from a mailing of 10,000 that results in a big dollar sale is a success—and the percentage of return was only 1/100th of 1 percent!

The basic percentage of return that will spell success for you relies on many variables including the product or service offered, the audience, the cost of the product/service, timing, frequency of mailing and the type of response you need.

Example: You buy an expensive camera. You fill out the warranty card. You mail it to the manufacturer. They sell or rent your name to a publisher who happens to have a book on how to use the camera you just bought.

The publisher can expect substantially better results from a mailing to a recent camera buyer than from a mailing for the same book to a list of photography magazine subscribers.

Similarly, a local photographer specializing in wedding photography can expect better results from a mailing to a list of recently engaged girls than from an "occupant" mailing in the area he covers.

Some products really need to be demonstrated, seen, felt, heard, to be effectively sold by mail and consequently would have a very low response rate. *The product itself makes the difference.*

The postcard from an accounting service could predictably be expected to do better when mailed just before the income tax deadline than as a general offering of accounting services at another time of the year. Timing makes the difference.

The response you want might not be an order. Perhaps you need only qualified leads for a salesperson to follow up. Or you might want to develop a refined mailing list for further mailings with more specific offers.

The type of response makes the difference.

Often, probably too often, first-time users of direct mail are disappointed with their results—they didn't meet the mythical anticipated return. And they give up direct mail. ("I tried it. It doesn't work . . .") What a shame!

A prime axiom for the direct mail user is "keep everlastingly at it." McGraw-Hill tells us the average industrial sale is made only after five calls by a salesperson. Isn't your direct mail a salesperson that needs to make a few calls to be effective.

Frequency makes the difference.

The criteria to determine what will make your mailing successful depends on how great a response is necessary to be profitable, either in terms of actual orders or an other measure of profitability.

That response is somewhere between the 1/100th of 1 percent for the computer manufacturer to 100 percent for the lavish-party giver.

How Do You Know if Your Direct Mail Is Profitable?

The same way you know if your business is profitable. You add up your costs and expenses. You subtract these from your income. If the number is on the plus side, you win.

Here's how it works with your direct mail.

1. Put down how many mailers you mailed.
2. Put down how much the total mailing cost for printing and postage.
3. Put down how much business you did.

If you have that information, you can now measure the success of your mailing.

Here's an example:

• You mail 1,000 letters

- Your unit cost: 30¢ for each letter (postage plus printing)
- Your total cost: $300 (30¢ x 1,000)
- You receive 50 orders (that's a 5 percent return)
- TOTAL OF ORDERS IS $1,000.
- YOUR TOTAL GROSS PROFIT IS: $500.
- YOUR COST: —300.

   CONCLUSION: You made . . . . $200. . . . on this mailing.

This is a very, very simple example. Sometimes your budget can be much more complicated. How do you figure in bad debts? Other advertising? Financing? Returns? If your direct mail begins to become *that* complicated, think of using a computer (see Chapter 14) not only for mailings but also for information about your mailings.

One of the masters of direct marketing math and finance is Pierre Passavant, an international speaker and former circulation manager of J. C. Penney and Vice President of Xerox Education Publications. Working with Judy Quick, whose background is computer software, the team has produced a direct marketing promotion budget on PC software.

For more information on their program write them at:

Passavant & Quick
193 Main Street
P. O. Box 1206
Middletown, CT 06457

Refining Your Response

Once you establish a response rate based on actual mailings, you are ready to take the next step—*testing.*

The fate of large mailers rests with testing. Before they mail millions of pieces they must be reasonably sure of their anticipated results. Fortunately there are formulas and charts based on statistics and the laws of probability that will give them help.

As a do-it-yourself mailer you often do not get concerned with extensive testing. But even the small mailer should test one or more of these important elements:

1. *The product.* You may really believe people are ready for this new item from you. You may find they could not care less.

2. *The list.* If you are selling an insurance program for non-smokers and you send your package to smokers you will have a bad response. Good offer, wrong list. If you are selling toys for the new baby and you mail the offer to senior citizens, you might reach a few grandparents who want to buy, but you have chosen the wrong list.

3. *The offer.* You will quickly discover if the price is too high. The quantity too large. The quantity too small. What are the product features? Size, shape, weight, material, workmanship, where made, by whom, colors, guarantee and price. The key, of course, is to simply make the readers an offer they can't refuse.

Doubleday increased their mail order sales of books when they simply changed the headline from "Buy four books for only one dollar" to "Buy three books for only one dollar and the fourth book is free!"

4. *Creativity.* Did anyone read your ad? Why? (See Chapter 6, Off with Their Head.)

5. *The timing.* More people buy by mail in January. Perhaps it's the money received at Christmas. Perhaps it's the guilt from the gift forgotten and suddenly remembered. Perhaps it's people being home because of the weather. Whatever the reason there are millions of letters arriving in mailboxes all over this country in January from Publisher's Clearing House to *Reader's Digest* and more—all testifying to the fact that this is *the* time to mail your offer. (See TOOLBOX.)

Timing: Catching a fad on its way up is a good idea, but if you miss you can wind up with a warehouse full of hula hoops and Nehru jackets.

Now . . . after you find that one letter, that one offer, that one product that captures the imagination and the pocketbook of your customer, fine. Keep on using it.

But also keep on trying, to a small section of your mailing list with yet *another* way to sell this merchandise.

Another phrase, another price, another method of payment.

Basic testing consists of establishing a control package with a known response. Now, vary the elements of the package to see if a revised version will out-pull the control. This fundamental approach eliminates the need for complicated mathematics. Your first mailing may serve as the control and subsequent mailings in their entirety may be considered the test sample.

Don Williams of Williams Air, a small New Jersey charter air service built entirely on direct mail and referrals from direct mail customers, mails 2,500 to 10,000 pieces to prospects in a 75-mile area. Each mailing serves as a test against his first effort or control. He tested lists and found some lists continually out-produce others—and his business grew. Then he tested *appeal* changes. A convenience-oriented mailing out-pulled a safety-oriented mailing. He tested letters *vs.* self-mailers and offers of free gifts to frequent charterers *vs.* discounted rates. His results got better and better.

What Not to Test

For the do-it-yourselfer there is the danger of testing the wrong things or too many things. Many things have already been tested and proven.

Typically, we know what months are best for mailing for certain businesses and appeals.

What color stamps to use is a meaningless test for the smaller direct mail user since the results are insignificant. Leave the testing of minor changes to the big mailers. Concentrate on one or more of the five variables previously listed.

Keying Your Test

When you split your mailing and test one half against another or split your mailing list to test one portion against another, you need some way to recognize the source of your response. Mailers can code their reply address by adding keys such as department numbers or persons' names, or slight modifications in return addresses.

Record Keeping

Testing not only lets you know which mailing package produces the best result but also tells you why one package out produces another. The "why" factor needs to be identified and recorded.

Keep a record of how many pieces were mailed, when, and the responses listed by number with the dates they were received. Attach a copy of the mailing to the tabulation sheet for future comparison of results.

Is Anybody Really Listening (Or Reading)

Direct mail, unlike most other media, is extremely measurable. You send your advertising to selected groups. Do they open it? Do they read it? Do they respond?

How *many* respond is the ultimate test.

The thought and preparation and homework done before the mailing will probably have more effect on the results from the changes resulting from testing. Combining careful preparation with testing will have your mailings opened, read, acted on. And the cash register repeatedly opened *ad profitum!*

TOOLBOX

When is the best *time* to mail?

Two answers.

1. Tests have proven certain months give a better response to mailings than any other month.

2. Further refined tests prove that certain *products* have certain months that pull better.

First things first.

Direct Marketing Association (DMA) has charted direct mail response by months. This is a good guide for when direct mail pulls best:

MONTH	COMPARATIVE	MONTH	COMPARATIVE
January	100%	July	73.3%
February	96.3%	August	87.0%
March	71.0%	September	79.9%
April	71.5%	October	89.9%
May	71.5%	November	81.0%
June	67.0%	December	79.0%

But the Kleid Company, one of the top list brokers in the United States, says you also have to consider your business. If you're in business or finance, the three top months seem to be January, December and September. If you are selling books, December, July and January are very good. Here are some other groupings and the months they found best to mail over a five-year average:

Self Improvement: December, January, July. (Nearly half the products and services sold on self improvement are sold in these months.

Parents and Children: January, July, December, August, February. (More than 74 percent of the results in just these five months.)

Hobbies: July and December.

Entertainment: December, January and July.

Fund Raising: September, October, January.

Note: December and January rank in the top four best months in nine out of ten categories.

What kind of a return should you expect?

Here's a probability list from direct mail expert, Ray Jutkins in California.*

If the size of the test mailing is:	and the return on the last mailing is:	then 95 chances out of 100, return on identical mailings to whole list will be between:
2,000	1%	.55/1.45%
2,000	2%	1.37/2.63%
2,000	3%	2.24/3.76%
2,000	4%	3.12/4.88%
2,000	5%	4.03/5.97%
2,000	10%	8.66/11.34%
2,000	20%	18.21/21.70%
10,000	1%	.80/1.20%
10,000	2%	1.72/2.28%
10,000	3%	2.66/3.34%
10,000	4%	3.61/4.39%
10,000	5%	4.56/5.44%
10,000	10%	9.40/10.60%
10,000	20%	19.20/20.80%

State of the Art

The best states in direct mail response are Alaska; Washington, D. C.; Hawaii; California; Nevada; Arizona; Wyoming. The least responsive are Mississippi, Massachusetts and Alabama. These figures are from Ray Snyder, DM consultant and former sales manager of the direct mail department of *World Book* and quoted in Bob Stone's *excellent* book *Successful Direct Marketing Methods*.

Finally . . .

In testing, you should know the Reasons Why people buy. Ed Mayer, whom we've referred to often in these pages, came up with a list of 26 reasons people buy. Everytime we come up with a new one we find it is already on his list . . .

When you are testing your letter or offer in the mail, look it over and

*Jutkins sends an attractive mail package out to potential clients that revolves around his "team." And so he uses baseball cards, but instead of the past and present greats on the major league teams, you receive pictures of Ray and his team members on their own baseball cards.

Write for a sample of this attractive mailing package. And ask if he has any more copies of this "More than 444 Begged, Borrowed, Stolen & Even a few Original! Direct Response Marketing IDEAS." It's a 55-page *Reader's Digest* condensed version of the basic facts and figures on direct response. His address: Ray Jutkins, 2121 Cloverfield Boulevard, Santa Monica, CA 90404. Tell him Murray and Ken sent you.

see how many of these reasons why are included in your mailing piece. The more you have, the higher the rate of your success.

1. To make money
2. To save money
3. To save time
4. To avoid effort
5. To get more comfort
6. To achieve greater cleanliness
7. To attain fuller health
8. To escape physical pain
9. To gain praise
10. To be popular
11. To attract the opposite sex
12. To conserve possessions
13. To increase enjoyment
14. To gratify curiosity
15. To protect family
16. To be in style
17. To have or hold beautiful possessions
18. To satisfy appetite
19. To emulate others
20. To avoid trouble
21. To avoid criticism
22. To be individual
23. To protect reputation
24. To take advantage of opportunities
25. To have safety in buying something else
26. To make work easier

The P.S.

In Conclusion . . .

Old H. L. Hunt rarely gave interviews.

The Texas multi-billionaire kept his own counsel. He rarely returned phone calls from the media to discuss business.

One day a local radio station talk show host persuaded him to come on his program. During the conversation the interviewer asked, "What's the secret of success?"

Old H. L. thought about that for a moment and then replied. Within a few days his answer was picked up from this small Texas radio station and found its way into national media coverage. Here is what he said: "There are only four things you have to do to be successful. Here they are:

"*One:* Decide what you want to do.

"*Two:* Decide what you'll give up to get it.

"*Three:* Decide your priorities.

"*Four:* Get on about your work."

At this point we hope you've passed step one and have decided that you *do* want to use direct mail to increase your business.

Step Two is interesting (and we have never read that one before in all the How-to-Succeed books) because it says you must *give up* something to succeed: leisure time/entertainment/another possession—a sacrifice must be made to ensure success.

Step Three is what you have read up to this point.

And Step Four is what you do after you finish this sentence . . .

APPENDIX I
Tools for the Toolbox

If you've ever been involved in any kind of do-it-yourself project, you know the job is easier and better if you have the right tools.

You do not have to spend a lot of money to create a successful direct mail piece!

Be it a simple postcard, a letter, a brochure, a self-mailer or even a basic catalog, there are ways you can cut costs.

We've collected some tools for your toolbox that will come in handy for do-it-yourself readers—those who will actually put together a mailing in house for delivery to the printer.

Artist's Supplies

For almost everything imaginable in artist supplies write or phone for a catalog from:

Dick Blick
P. O. Box 1267
Galesburg, IL 61401
309/343-6181

Arthur Brown & Sons
2 West 46th Street
New York, NY 10036
212/575-5544

Transfer Type

An inexpensive and convenient way to paste up headlines for envelopes, letters and brochures is to use transfer type. This consists of alphabets and numbers in a wide variety of type styles and sizes on clear plastic sheets. The letters can be transferred to paper by rubbing with a burnishing tool or stylus. Another form of transfer type requires the letter be cut from acetate sheets and laid down with self-adhering adhesive. Information on these products is available from:

FORMAT GRAPHIC PRODUCTS CORP.
Rolling Meadow, IL 60008

CHARTPAC
Leeds, MA 01053

LETRASET U.S.A., INC.
40 Eisenhower Drive
Paramus, NJ 07652

Envelope Information

Several of the major envelope makers have valuable free information available, with particular emphasis on direct mail. Refer to your local classified directory for envelope distributors who may have this material. Or write:

BOSTON ENVELOPE
31 Middlesex Road
Mainsfield, MA 02048

BOISE CASCADE ENVELOPES
313 Rohlwing Road
Addison, IL 60101

TENSION ENVELOPE CORPORATION
819 East 19th Street
Kansas City, MI 64108

WESTVACO (US Envelope Division)
Advertising Department
P. O. Box 3300
Springfield, MA

Paper

The "look" and "feel" of your mailing makes a significant difference in readership and results. You do not have to use white paper all the time.
Like the envelope companies, many of the major paper manufacturers will provide you with swatch kits and helpful literature. But . . . go first to your local sources in the telephone directory. If you have no luck, write to:

APPLETON PAPERS
Division of NCR
Appleton, WI 54911

THE BECKETT PAPER COMPANY
Hamilton, OH 45012

FINCH, PRUYN AND COMPANY, INC.
Glens Falls, NY 12801

FRENCH PAPER COMPANY
Niles, MI 49120

GEORGIA-PACIFIC CORPORATION
Hopper Paper Division
Reading, PA 19603

GILBERT PAPER COMPANY
A Mead Company
Menasha, WI 54952

HAMMERMILL PAPER COMPANY
Erie, PA 16533

MEAD PAPER
Dayton, OH 45463

MOHAWK PAPER MILLS, INC.
Cohoes, NY 12047

NEKOOSA PAPERS, INC.
A company of
Great Northern Nekoosa Corporation
Port Edwards, WI 54469

OLD COLONY ENVELOPE COMPANY
Westfield, MA 01085/Dayton, OH 45463

PARSONS PAPER
Division NVF Company
Holyoke, MA 01040

RIEGEL PRODUCTS CORP.
A Subsidiary of
Southern Forest Industries
Milford, NJ 08848

STRATHMORE PAPER COMPANY
Westfield, MA 01085

UNION CAMP CORPORATION
Franklin, VA 23851

S. D. WARREN COMPANY
A Division of Scott Paper Company
Boston, MA 02101

WAUSAU PAPER MILLS COMPANY
Brokaw, WI 54417

Stock Art

Thousands of line drawings, illustrations, borders, symbols, cover designs, newsletter formats, etc., are available to be cut out (clip art) and pasted on to your mechanical. Among the best known sources are:

ARTMASTER•ART-PAK
550 N. Claremont Blvd.
Claremont, CA 91711

DYNAMIC GRAPHICS
P. O. Box 1901
Peoria, IL 61656-1901

VOLK CLIP ART, INC.
P. O. Box 72
Pleasantville, NJ 08232

Stock Bulletin Forms

For sales letters, announcements and newsletter you can get preprinted letters and envelopes with humorous themes done in color. All you have to do is add your own identification and message in black and white.

CARR SPEIRS
24 Rope Ferry Road
Waterford, CT 06386

A note of caution concerning do-it-yourself graphics: be careful when you borrow. There's always a strong temptation to borrow art, headlines and even photos from other publications. Remember most material is copyrighted. "Borrowing" can lead to legal problems. The original user probably paid handsomely for his graphics and is not anxious to subsidize your efforts.

Stock Photographs

Similar to stock art, stock photographs, either in black and white or color, can be purchased for one time use. A complete listing of almost all of the stock photo suppliers can be found in the *Photographers Market Annual,* published by Writers Digest Books, 9933 Alliance Road, Cincinnati, OH 45252. Among the major sources are:

HAROLD M. LAMBERT STUDIOS, INC.
Box 27310
Philadelphia, PA 19150

PHOTOWORLD, INC.
251 Park Avenue South
New York, NY 10010

H. ARMSTRONG ROBERTS
4203 Locust Street
Philadelphia, PA 19104

RICHARDS COMMERCIAL PHOTO SERVICE
732 Pacific Avenue
Tacoma, WA 98402

Addressing and Postal Equipment

In addition to addressing by computers there is other addressing equipment available. For those who may want to meter their mail or use stamps, major suppliers of this equipment are:

SCRIPTOMATIC, INC.
1 Scriptomatic Plaza
Philadelphia, PA 19131

JENKIN SECURITY
Suite 7, 13th Floor
77 Pacific Highway
North Sydney, N.S.W.
Australia 2060

ADDRESSOGRAPPH MULTIGRAPH CORP.
1200 Babbitt Road
Cleveland, OH 44117

STAMP MASTER
18525 Sherman Way
Los Angeles, CA 91335

INTERNATIONAL MAILING SYSTEMS
8 Brook Street
P. O. Box 858
Shelton, CT 06484

POSTMATIC, INC.
2665 Fourth Avenue
Anoka, MN 55303

PITNEY BOWES, INC.
Walter H. Wheeler Jr. Drive
Stanford, CT 06926

Mailing List Information

Several of the leasing mailing list brokers have booklets and news letters with helpful information for direct mailers. Write to:

DIRECT MARKETING GROUP, INC.
33 Irving Place
New York, NY 10003

THE KLEID COMPANY
200 Park Avenue
New York, NY 10166

GEORGE-MANN ASSOCIATES INC.
403 Mercer Street
Hightstown, NJ 08520

WOODRUFF-STEVENS
345 Park Avenue South
New York, NY 10166

United States Government

A great source for a wide variety of information booklets of advertising and direct mail is the U.S. Small Business Administration. Write them at:

1441 "L" Street
Wsahington, DC 20416

Free photographs are available from most government agencies pending on the subject material needed. The Library of Congress is another source for free photographs by writing to:

Library of Congress
10 First St. S.E.
Washington, DC 20540

Ready?
Get set . . .
GO!

APPENDIX II
Join the Club!

Regional U.S. Direct Marketing Clubs and Contacts

1. Chicago Association of Direct Marketing
600 South Federal, Suite 400
Chicago, IL 60605
Phone: (312) 346-1600
President: Robert Marinello
Number of members: 2,200

2. Direct Marketing Association of Indianapolis
c/o Sales and Research Corp.
6119 Guion Road
Indianapolis, IN 46254
Phone: (317) 253-4321
Chairman: Tom Bowers
Number of members: 50

3. Direct Marketing Association of Detroit
35540 W. Michigan Ave., Suite 206
Wayne, MI 48234
Phone: (313) 721-0990
President: Robert Breese
Number of members: 750

4. Direct Marketing Association of North Texas
P.O. Box 612368
D-SW Airport, Texas 75261
Phone: (817) 640-7018
President: Bob Daniels
Number of members: 425

5. Direct Marketing Association of Tulsa
c/o Kraftbilt
P.O. Box 800
Tulsa, OK 74101
Phone: (800) 331-7290
President: Mike Goldberg
Number of members: 30

6. Mid-South Direct Marketing Association
c/o Fitzpatrick Associates
8500 Hunters Horn
Germantown, TN 38138
Phone: (901) 756-5369
President: Allan Katz
Number of members: 20

7. Direct Marketing Association of St. Louis
12686 Lonsdale Dr.
Bridgeton, MO 63044
Phone: (314) 291-7405
President: Pamela Hutchings
Number of members: 500

8. Houston Direct Marketing Association
1002 Texas Parkway
Stafford, TX 77477
Phone: (713) 499-0417
President: Ron Moran
Number of members: 140

9. Direct Marketing Club of New York
224 Seventh St.
Garden City, NY 11530
Phone: (516) 746-6700
President: Ralph Stevens
Number of members: 1,114

10. Direct Marketing Club of Southern California
2401 Pacific Coast Highway
Suite 206
Hermosa Beach, CA 90254
Phone: (213) 374-7499
President: Buzz Brown
Number of members: 450

11. Direct Response Advertising and Marketing Association of Hawaii
c/o Tropical Rent-A-Car Systems, Inc.
550 Paiea Street - Suite 201
Honolulu, HI 96819-1895
Phone: (808) 836-0788
President: David Erdman
Number of members: 140

12. Florida Direct Marketing Association
P.O. Box 4550
South Daytona, FL 32021
Phone: (904) 756-0060
President: Robert Long
Number of members: 450

13. Direct Marketing Association of Washington
655 15th St. N.W., Suite 300
Washington, DC 20005
Phone: (202) 347-MAIL
President: William Armisted
Number of members: 1,300

14. Mid-America Direct Marketing Association
P.O. Box 3651
Omaha, NE 68103-0651
Phone: (402) 734-4442
President: Gary Parker
Number of members: 250

15. Midwest Direct Marketing Association
P.O. Box 2353, Loop Station
Minneapolis, MN 55402
Phone: (612) 470-0197
President: Rollie Lange
Number of members: 600

16. Long Island Direct Marketing Association
c/o Fulfillment Plus, Inc.
1626-8 Locust Avenue
Bohemia, NY 11716
Phone: (516) 563-2250
President: Howard Erlich
Number of members: 110

17. Louisville Direct Marketing Association
c/o Personnel Policy Service Inc.
P.O. Box 7715
Louisville, KY 40207
Phone: (502) 897-6782
President: Lynn Sponholz
Number of members: 90

18 San Diego Direct Marketing Club
c/o Allen M. Greer & Associates
1081 Camina del Rio South
Suite 238
Phone: (619) 298-8335
President: Allen Greer
Number of members: 200

19. Hudson Valley Direct Marketing Club
c/o 455 Central Ave., Suite 315
Scarsdale, NY 10583
Phone: (914) 723-3176
President: Bob Foehl
Number of members: 50

20. Maryland Direct Marketing Association
34 Somers Court
Cockeyville, MD 21030
Phone: (301) 628-2450
President: Doug McRay
Number of members: 130

21. New England Direct Marketing Association
70 Walnut Street
Wellesly, MA 02181
Phone: (617) 239-8238
President: Steven Tharler
Number of members: 450

22. Northeast Ohio Direct Mail and Marketing Association
Statler Office Tower, Suite 303
Cleveland, OH 44115
Phone: (216) 241-8188
President: John Klein
Number of members: 200

23. Ohio Valley Direct Marketing Club
c/o Cincinnati Bell
201 East Fourth Street
Phone: (513) 397-1555
President: Silvia Jarvis
Number of members: 130

24. Direct Marketing Association of Orange County
P.O. Box 16473
Irvine, CA 92713
Phone: (714) 380-9100
President: Robert Groag
Number of members: 165

25. Phoenix Direct Marketing Club
P.O. Box 8756
Phoenix, AZ 85006
Phone: (602) 268-5237
President: Julie Everson
Number of members: 210

26. Philadelphia Direct Marketing Association
190 S. Warner Rd., Suite 100
Wayne, PA 19087
Phone: (215) 688-5040
President: Joan Ryan
Number of members: 800

27. Rocky Mountain Direct Marketing Association
P.O. Box 1784
Boulder, CO 80111
Phone: (303) 220-8789
President: Susan Fantle
Number of members: 180

28. Oregon Direct Marketing Association
c/o PSW Direct
319 S. W. Washington, 11th Floor
Portland, OR 97204
Phone: (503) 279-4000
Number of members: 450

29. Kansas City Direct Marketing Association
P.O. Box 41133
Kansas City, MO 64141
Phone: (816) 472-0880
President: Larry Hawks
Number of members: 400

30. Seattle Direct Marketing Association
217 9th Avenue North
Seattle, WA 98109
Phone: (206) 284-1755
President: Steve Saunders
Number of members: 130

31. Southeast Direct Marketing Association
c/o Ace Mailing Services
1961 Cobb Industrial Blvd.
Smyrna, GA 30080
Phone: (404) 434-5757
President: Bill Smith
Number of members: 378

32. Spokane Direct Mail Association
c/o Books in Motion
East 9212 Montgomery, Suite 504
Spokane, WA 99206
Phone: (509) 922-1646
President: Gary Challender
Number of members: 51

33. Upstate New York Direct Marketing Association
c/o The Sutherland Group
2023 W. Henrietta Road
Rochester, NY 14623
Phone: (716) 272-8400
President: Scott Seeman
Number of members: 80

34. Wisconsin Direct Marketing Club
c/o National Business Furniture
222 East Michigan Street
Milwaukee, WI
Phone: (414) 377-3355
President: George Mosher
Number of members: 160

35. San Francisco Advertising Club
150 Post Street
San Francisco, CA 94108
Phone: (415) 986-3878
Chairman, Direct Response Group:
Mary Donohue
Number of members: 350

APPENDIX III
Direct Marketing Flow Chart

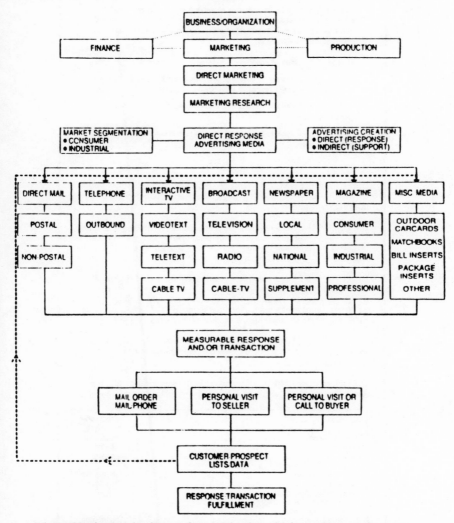

Direct Marketing is the total activities by which products and services are offered to market segments in one or more media for informational purposes and/or to solicit a direct response from a present or prospective customer, or contributor, by mail, telephone or personal visit.

MARTIN BAIER, HENRY R. HOKE, JR., ROBERT STONE
November 7, 1978

DIRECT MARKETING - What Is It?

An Aspect of Total Marketing - not a fancy term for mail order.

Marketing is the total of activities of moving goods and services from seller to buyer. (See chart). Direct Marketing has the same broad function except that Direct Marketing requires the existence and maintenance of database.

a) to record names of customers, expires and prospects.

b) to provide a vehicle for storing, then measuring, results of advertising, usually direct response advertising.

c) to provide a vehicle for storing, then measuring, purchasing performance.

d) to provide a vehicle for continuing direct communication by mail and/or phone.

THUS

DIRECT MARKETING is interactive, requiring database for controlled activity: By mail, by phone, through other media selected on the basis of previous results.

DIRECT MARKETING makes direct response advertising generally desirable since response (inquiries or purchasing transactions) can be recorded on database for building the list, providing marketing information.

DIRECT MARKETING plays no favorites in terms of Methods of Selling...and there are only three:
a) Where buyer seeks out seller - retailing, exhibits
b) Where seller seeks out buyer - personal selling
c) Where buyer seeks seller by mail or phone - mail order

DIRECT MARKETING requires that a response or transaction at any location be recorded on cards, mechanical equipment or, preferably, on computer.

DIRECT MARKETING can be embraced by any kind of business as defined by the U.S. Census Standard Industrial Classification system:

Agriculture	0100-0999
Mining/Construction	1000-1799
Manufacturing	2000-4999
Wholesale	5010-5199
Retail	5210-5999
Department Stores (5311)	
Financial Services	6010-6799
Services	7010-7999
Advertising Agencies (7311)	
Computer Houses (7372)	
List Brokers (7388)	
Non-Profit	8010-8999
Public Administration	9100-9999

DIRECT MARKETING is an interactive system of marketing which uses one or more advertising media to effect a measurable response and/or transaction at any location.